"Terry's book is truly a gem in christian literature, maybe because he is not a "professional" focused on wordings more than message. It is open-minded, upfront, honest, and leads the reader by the hand through the pages."

Thomas Lardon - *Lardon Media, Berlin, Germany*

"What a great read. DISCIPLED, by Terry Clark, reminds us: if salvation is the gift of God, discipleship is what happens next. Insightful and honest, DISCIPLED is not just a great read, it elegantly describes how we are conformed to God's expectation through the mentorship of Holy Scripture. Read the book. Be surprised."

Floyd Wray-*Writer/Animator/Software Design at MBooks*

"Terry takes us on a journey through Matthew, focusing on Jesus' words — the red letters. His commentary is full of wisdom and insight honed by years of studying God's Word and time spent in God's presence. DISCIPLED is a treasure."

Carol Loughlin - *Retired Executive Director of the Texas Municipal League Intergovernmental Risk Pool*

To Ken -
Beloved Friend,
confidant & brother
in Christ! Happy.
Birthday - Love, Bill

THANKS!

There has been an incredible team enthusiastically working long and hard to make this project become what it was meant to be.

My wife, **Nancy**, heads the list.
Without her gracious instincts and amazing proofing skill, honestly, this wouldn't be happening.

My daughter, **Renee Story**, Graphic Designer and Ancient History Buff.
Renee is not only responsible for the graphic design of the cover but also the entire layout of the book. She was also, along with Nancy, one of the first encouragements to take my study of Matthew's Gospel to print.

Floyd Wray, my friend since boyhood and duet partner on the giant marimba.
I contacted Floyd to tell him about this accidental book I had written and ask him if he could give any pointers. At every challenge, he was an enormous force of wisdom, encouragement and enthusiasm.

There are many other long-time friends and family that we have shared this endeavor with. Each and every one has been a perfectly fitted piece of a beautiful puzzle that now is available to hold in your hands.

TABLE OF CONTENTS

FOREWORD

What a great read. *DISCIPLED*, by Terry Clark, reminds us: salvation is the gift of God, but discipleship is what happens next.

For many, after accepting God's gift of redemption at the cross, nothing else is required, nothing can be taken away, and nothing remains to be done. Of course, this is not quite true. Christ died for us; but we are to live for Him. How to live for Him presents us with an ongoing challenge. This is where most of us are in dire need of discipling.

By the way, a covenant is God's bottom-line for dealing with the human family. It's often expressed as an if-then proposition. A good example is found in 2 Chronicles 7:14.

> *If my people, which are called by my name, shall humble themselves, and pray, and seek my face, and turn from their wicked ways; then will I hear from heaven, and forgive their sin, and will heal their land.*

Christ's covenantal expectation, found in John 14:15, is a bit more succinct.

> *If you love me, (then) keep my commandments.*

Keeping Christ's commandments is what we're supposed do. By such measure we are thus redeemed and reformed (or discipled). Through the counsel of God's Word, and the example set by our Savior, our lives are to be mentored in righteousness.

As I reviewed early drafts of *DISCIPLED*, I was touched to see such a poignant snapshot of the human condition. Having known Terry most of my life, I was aware of the challenges he endured. It didn't surprise me to find his honesty linked so closely to an emphasis on discipleship–this is how he survived. I was the one who drove him to the recruiting station the night he entered military service. In the years that followed, I saw, first-hand, his spiritual challenges. I witnessed my childhood friend, Terry Clark, as he became the poster boy for survival-by-discipleship.

His book is honest and direct, and written by someone who fully understands the connection between redemption and reformation. If any of us are to survive this "tough life" of ours, we'd be well-advised to pursue the challenge of being discipled. *How Does A New Creature Act?* (the title for Chapter 3), takes a hard focus on how we are to pursue new life in Christ. Ultimately, discipling is all about having your life curated by Godly counsel.

In *MERE CHRISTIANITY*, C.S. Lewis wrote: "each day we are becoming a creature of splendid glory or one of unthinkable horror." *DISCIPLED* encourages our pursuit of this splendid glory. Insightful and honest, it's not just a great read, it elegantly describes how we are conformed to God's expectation through Holy Scripture and godly example. Read the book. Be ... surprised by joy.

Floyd Wray,
Author of *LIFEPLANNING, BLOOD TOYS,* and
THE BATTLE OF THE ALAMO (An Augmented Reality Book)

PRESTORY

I grew up hearing God's words among people who believed that if God said it, that settles it. They lived their lives as an open experiment in the application of God's revelation about His creation and who His people are to be.

At the center, were those *red letters*, the words of Jesus; this Son of God, Son of Man, the Word and love of God in human flesh, our connection to a reality; a world of joy forever. My earliest memories are His words. *"For God so loved..."*

I knew the words and had a level of understanding, even as a young boy, from personal conversations with Him. My first pastors and gospel influences were members of my own family. My grandmother, Bessie Quillin-Harrell, was a fire-breathing preacher who had been filled and possessed by the heart, mind and passion of God in the early 20th Century outpouring of His Holy Spirit in America. Her brother, my great-uncle, Leon Quillin, was pastor of the church where, as a child, I was immersed in all it means to be a community of believers. But in public school, I learned to be a chameleon, to take the shape and personality of whatever group I fell in with.

My adaptability developed to expert level by the time I was drafted into the Army. Already several friends had come back from Vietnam in boxes or with missing parts. So, when I reported for the draft, my determination was to enlist, instead of the short training-to-body-bag soldier mill. I was offered a military intelligence job that was pitched in a way that couldn't be turned down. Then I headed for a 4-year long, multi-destination path, getting a deep education in the cultures, experiences and entanglements possible on this globe. Japan, Southeast Asia, and several US installations that were just as foreign to me, were on that path.

I arrived at my sixth and final deployment in southern Germany, a very tired and burned-out young man, with a wife and a baby girl. To learn another language or adapt to another culture had absolutely no allure. I worked, doted over my daughter as she turned a year-old and played tourist with a group of friends whose common bond had nothing to do with my up-bringing.

Late one night, after a no-win battle with my superiors, plus some confusing rifts with my wife, I sat at the dining table alone, in the dark, while the girls slept soundly in the next room. There, I gathered my entire life in a pile and took inventory, looking, I suppose, for value in anything beyond that tiny, sleeping almost-one-year-old in the other room.

The unavoidable conclusion was that there could not be anything more completely shameful and humiliating than being a member of the human race. I'd seen all that humans are capable of and participated in more than I would want to admit to. I left my whole life piled on that table to be taken out with the morning's garbage and stepped across a little picket fence that marked the boundary of this world's definition of sanity. A little while later the van arrived and men in white jackets came to take me away.

Lying in my room on the psych floor of the military hospital in Munich, after a "No Hope" diagnosis, I heard a familiar voice. No, I was not hallucinating, though they were giving me more drugs than I'd ever taken before. I recognized the voice of my childhood friend. Jesus said, *"Terry, I know how you feel. I've seen everything humans have ever done. And believe me, I'm grossed out too. But I want you to see the difference in our response to that shameful truth. You have decided not to be a human being. I chose to become one."*

He then flooded me with how He feels toward human beings. I was drowned in a passion that instantly eclipsed the disgust and humiliation. It filled my emptied shell of a soul and plunged me into fathomless depths of a love that I could have never imagined.

"Now, Terry, what do you want to do? Which will you choose? It's up to you."

For the first time I understood *why* the cross. It was always real to me, but now I could taste it. Now, the choice was just a technicality. Jesus had just given me the only rational reason to be a human being I had heard as an adult. His. I wanted back in the game.

The change was very physical. Jesus had swept away the ashes of a burned-out brain and replaced it with a fresh one. With a new mind, my body started going through a radical transformation and that day, my diagnosis was changed from *"No Hope,"* to *"Recovering Satisfactorily,"* and within the week, they sent me home.

But... during the week, in the midst of checking my reflexes and cutting the dosage of the drugs they were giving me, something happened that made it clear forever how serious the situation really had been. A night-shift head nurse came to work after vacation and went about her usual duties. Reviewing the charts from the previous night, she filled her pill cups, loaded her cart and started her rounds. However, the doctor had slashed the dosage so many times on the current day's chart, more than likely, there was nothing left for the evening dose. She had filled my cup with the 21 pastel pills they had been giving me three times a day. It wasn't long after swallowing those pills that I began to feel very strange. I pushed off the bed and made my way around to the nurses' station. She glanced up at me and grabbed the phone. Soon the doctor arrived with a very large syringe and the antidote that kept me from turning into a rock with a nice new brain inside.

I did not walk out of the hospital like Superman coming out of a phone booth. It was a completely new start for me, with a brand new brain to learn how to live again. Everything was new. From that day Jesus is my only sanity, and if asked why, my answer is the same as Peter's. *"Where else would I go? Jesus, You alone have the words of life."*

I am still RECOVERING SATISFACTORILY. Each day's expedition through new vistas into Him and mind-blowing discovery has been and continues to be my most difficult challenge, eclipsed by a mounting joy I could have never imagined. Thank You, Jesus!

WHY READ MATTHEW'S JOURNAL?
Those who love me, do what I say.
(John 6:63, 8:51-52, 12:47, 14:15-23, 15:7, :10, :14, :20)

Well, then, what does He say? Jesus was not only the one who created human beings, but He also became one of us so that He could be our undisputed Authority on being a normal one.

When He walked the dusty roads of Judea, sat on the Mount of Olives and in a boat just off the shore of Galilee, the words He spoke were not high-sounding religious rhetoric. He spoke the common street Hebrew[1] of the workingman. Those are the people He came to speak to and, if we can step down into who we really are and look up to Him, we too will hear Him clearly.

His words are still *"Spirit and Life"* today (John 6:63). He is right here and speaks those words directly and personally to us as we read them. He put them down in His Book specifically for us and if we are really listening, they will truly be a *"lamp unto our feet"* (Ps 119:105).

As we discover the words of Jesus together, the most important question to keep in view is, "What is Jesus saying TO ME? How does that affect the way I will live?" So, we clear the clutter in our minds, push everything - whether good or bad - back to the walls, and ask Him to cleanse the temple. Now, we invite Him to take His rightful place on the throne of our hearts and set our focus to intently listen for and engage in His personal conversation with us. We open the ears of our hearts as He unfolds His perspective, and the eyes of our hearts as He shows us its personal application in our daily life, today. Then we follow, do whatever is called for and press toward Him, no matter what we have to leave behind.

Father, bless us as we read Matthew's personal journal as he became Your disciple, and with him, unwrap Your Words together. Give us courage to step through the thresholds You call us through, and the gumption during the process, to never see ourselves alone. You are with us, therefore we are together in You.

[1] Douglas Hamp, *DISCOVERING THE LANGUAGE OF JESUS,*
CC Publishing, Costa Mesa CA, 2005

Throughout, the Scripture references will be drawn from these translations:

ESV – English Standard Version, 2001 Crossway Bibles

AMPC – Amplified Classic Bible, 1965 Zondervan and The Lockman Foundation

AMP – Amplified Bible, 2015 revision Zondervan and The Lockman Foundation

[AMP/AMPC Bible is used to give wide-angle definitions]

NLT – New Living Translation, 1996, 2015 Tyndale

CJB – Complete Jewish Bible, 1998 David H. Stern

PHILLIPS – J.B. Phillips New Testament, 1960, 1972

Chapter One

THE FIRST RED LETTERS
Matthew 3:15

The first *red letters* are not the Sermon on the Mount, The Great Commission, The Lord's Prayer or even John 3:16. They are words spoken to John the Baptist and up until now may have seemed an unlikely opener. But, they are the first of His words we come to when we begin to read the New Testament and that could be a clue that they may be more important than we might think. Here are those first red letter words of Jesus: *"Permit it just now; for this is the fitting way for us to fulfill all righteousness* (Matt 3:15 AMP)."

LET WHAT BE SO? Jesus had come to John to be baptized. John protested. (We probably would have too!) John says, "You come to be baptized by ME? I should be baptized by YOU!

His feelings are justified; his position logical, but Jesus had come to do a specific job and this was part of it. So He responds very firmly to John's protest: *"Let it be so."* What is He really saying? In essence, Jesus says, "Allow this to happen", or "Set aside your way of thinking and just do it, so that we can accomplish all that the Father requires - so we can get the job done He sent us to do."

It would be good to note here that from those same lips, about three and a half years later just before He departs from that body, now bruised and broken, wounded and hanging on a cross, came these final words: ***"IT IS FINISHED!"***

Those words are found in John 19:30. We will also find Him speaking about finishing what His Father had given Him to do in John 5:36 and 17:4. Paul also talks about finishing in Acts 20:24, and 2Timothy 4:7: *"But my life is worth nothing to me unless I use it for finishing the work assigned me by the Lord Jesus—the work of telling others the Good News about the wonderful grace of God. I have run the great race, I have finished the course, I have kept the faith."*

AS FOR MYSELF...

Are we living our life with the goal of finishing what God has in mind for us? Have we put any real thought and prayer into exactly what it is that God wants to accomplish with us? What about gifts and talents and calling? How do we know all that? How do we find out for sure what the will of God is for our life?

Well, that process starts for us very much like it did for John the Baptist the day he baptized Jesus. We must set aside our way and determine to know God and follow Him – His way.

This does not mean doing something mystical or super-spiritual. It simply means that we must begin to give room for the fact that His way will be more than just different from ours. God clearly says, *"Inquire of the Lord while He is present, call upon Him when He is close at hand... For My thoughts are not your thoughts, and your ways are not My ways. This is the very word of the Lord. For as the heavens are higher than the earth, so are My ways higher than your ways and My thoughts than your thoughts"* (Isaiah 55:6-9).

In John 6:66-68, many followers were leaving Jesus and going back to their own pursuits. He turns to the twelve disciples and asks, *"Will you leave me too?"* Then speaking for all who truly love Him, Peter answers, *"Lord, where shall we go? Your words are words of eternal life."* That seems pretty courageous under the circumstances, but when we consider the absolute truth of Peter's words it becomes a simple matter of life or death.

Are we willing to launch out of what we think are "safe waters" and drop anchor in Him? To love Him and believe in Him, means to do just that. We are to daily lay aside the old us and allow ourselves to be possessed, filled by Him.

This filling is what water baptism is all about. When Jesus was obedient to this detail in His Father's design for Him, He laid down even His ways, thoughts, words and authority. God, the Son, laid aside all that He was, to carry out the wishes of His Father.

From that point, He only did that which He had seen His Father do and said only what He heard Him say, giving us the perfect example of the simple but powerful life of a disciple who KNOWS and DOES the will of God.

We can know what He wants - and He has provided all we will need to make sure we are able to do it!

It is interesting that in the Chronological Bible, the first red letters give basically the same message. They are Luke 2:49 – *And he said to them, "But why were you looking for me? Did you not know that I must be in my Father's house?" (PHILLIPS)*

Chapter Two

BE ATTITUDES part one - THE TEST
Matthew 4:4,7,10

[my paraphrase]

The TRUTH says: Man was not made a physical being only. Therefore his life cannot be sustained by physical food alone. Being primarily a spiritual creation, man must have the nutrition in every word that comes from God's mouth.

The TRUTH says: You shall not exasperate the Lord your God with silly faith games.

Get out of my sight, Satan! It is a written law for everything in this whole universe: YOU SHALL WORSHIP THE LORD YOUR GOD AND YOU SHALL SERVE HIM ONLY!

Temptation #1: You're Hungry?

"You don't have to stand for that. You're a child of the King and therefore you can have whatever you need! A King's kid isn't meant to be going hungry. You have the authority to turn that stone into a loaf of bread. Confess it with your mouth and it will happen!"

Sounds like a current message from a local pulpit, doesn't it? That is not where it originates. It was the first of the three categories of temptation launched at Jesus in the wilderness. According to Matthew 4:1, the Holy Spirit took Jesus into the desert, where He fasted for forty days. Then, He was hungry. At that point the temptations began. We'll talk about the significance of the categories later, but right now let's hear again Jesus' response to the tempter:

"TRUTH says: Man was not made a physical being only. Therefore his life cannot be sustained by physical food alone. Being primarily a spiritual creation, man must have the nutrition in every word that comes from *God's* mouth."

These words come from the mouth of the One who IS those words coming from God's mouth.

"The Word became flesh and dwelt among us" (John 1:14). *"He was with God. He was God. All things were made and came into existence through Him. Not one thing that exists came into being without Him"* (John 1:1-3).

So we can safely assume that He knows the ingredients and requirements associated with man, the pinnacle of God's creation. Here He is reminding the devil and announcing to all the earth that man is meant to draw his life directly from God. In John 1:13, He defines the child of God as one who *"owes their birth neither to bloods, nor to the will of the flesh (physical impulse), nor the will of a natural father, but to God."*

[NOTE re: Spiritual Nutrition and Mal-nutrition- If our spiritual eyes were opened and we looked at the multitudes who call themselves Christians today, what had been a well-fed, healthy looking group of people in the physical realm would suddenly look like a group from a fund-raising spot for the starving in a third-world country! The deceiver has been so successful in keeping Man's attention on his physical existence that we don't realize, just as the flesh needs food, so does the spirit. In fact, the parallel is much more grave than eating or not eating. Jesus' illustration shows us that the flesh can go 40 days without being fed, but the spirit cannot be alive at all, for even a moment, without God's Breath (Spirit).]

Temptation #2: Take A Flying Leap!

Matthew 4:5 records that Satan took Jesus to Jerusalem and made Him stand on the highest point of the temple, then said, "Go ahead. Throw yourself out into apparent destruction. Let's see if God is with you. He said He would take care of you, didn't He? Go for it!"

Jesus replies, "TRUTH says: You shall not exasperate the Lord your God with silly 'faith' games."

Jesus uses words directly from Deuteronomy 6:16, *"You shall not tempt and try the Lord your God, as you did at Massah."* (AMPC) In Exodus 17:7 God called the place Massah (proof) and Meribah (contention) where the Israelites tempted and tried the patience of the Lord saying, *"Is the Lord among us or not?"*

The commercial brand of faith regularly says, "Ask for a miracle! Expect a miracle! Plant the seed-faith for your miracle here!" And when we are walking through a dry place it is common to say, "Where are You, God? Why don't You do something to prove You are still with me?"

This perception of God and our relationship with Him is designed to erode genuine faith. In a moment of desperate worked-up "faith", we jump out into whim and impulse expecting "**IF** He is there", God will bear us up on wings of eagles.

Instead of learning a valuable lesson from what happens, we begin to doubt that God even exists when He lets us "eat the fruit of our deeds." God is either God, or He's not. And if He is, I wouldn't recommend insulting Him! We need to establish a true understanding of what real faith is. Start by reading Hebrews 11 - over and over if needed - until we get the point. And – don't become a trial to God!

[NOTE re: Proving God – "Proving God" is not a demand and a leap. If we are really interested in proving God, we will take the time to look into the Word and find out how it is done. Proving God begins with, and proceeds from, bent knees and a contrite heart. In Romans 12:1-2 we read, "*I appeal to you therefore, brethren, and beg of you in view of (all) the mercies of God, to make a decisive dedication of your bodies presenting all your members and faculties as a living sacrifice, holy (devoted, consecrated) and well pleasing to God, which is your reasonable (rational, intelligent) service and spiritual worship. Do not be conformed to this world - this age, fashioned after and adapted to its external, superficial customs. But be transformed (changed) by the entire renewal of your mind - by its new ideals and its new attitudes - so that you may* **prove** *for yourselves what is the good and acceptable and perfect will of God, even the thing which is good and acceptable and perfect in His sight for you.*" (AMPC)]**

Temptation #3: Worship me!

In Matthew 4:8 the devil takes Jesus to a high vista point and shows Him a panorama of the splendor of all the earth's kingdoms and says, "Look! All the glitter, all the wealth and beauty and power of all the kingdoms of the world, I'll give to you. Just submit to me and worship me!" To understand what Satan was suggesting, refer to the definition of "*spiritual worship*" in Romans 12:2. It will also give gravity to the forceful words of Jesus' response.

Here Jesus is offered an easier, yet still spiritual, way to buy back ALL that His hands had made. He didn't come to buy all of it back. He knew He was on the only path that would truly accomplish the Father's purpose – our redemption.

Jesus replies, "*Get out of my sight, Satan! It is a written law for everyone in this whole universe:* **you shall worship the Lord your God and you shall serve him only!**"

With these words Jesus finishes the necessary confrontation with Satan's almost ceremonial series of temptations. The devil must have at least suspected that it was useless to try to stumble the Son of God. For Jesus, it was simply part of what He had to endure. Like His first words to John concerning what seemed to John an unnecessary baptism, it was *"necessary in order to fulfill everything that righteousness demanded."*

That episode becomes a preliminary demonstration of what Jesus is about to teach verbally about the attitude of a child of God. The "Sermon on the Mount" was illustrated by Him, toe-to-toe with the most formidable foe to our walk in Christ - Satan himself. And it wasn't even a contest! In baseball terms: **Three up - Three down! Halleluyah!**

CATEGORIES OF TEMPTATION

Looking at the kinds of pitches he was throwing can give us some insight into the devil's tactics toward us. Here are his targets:

1. FLESH "Turn that stone into bread. Satisfy that hunger"

2. MIND "See if God is with you. Make Him prove it"

3. SPIRIT "All the power is yours if you worship me"

Man is a 3-part being: Body, Mind and Spirit. Satan has a tailor-made temptation for each part of us.

John tells us in 1 John 2:15-17, *"Do not love or cherish the world or the things that are in the world. If anyone loves the world, love for the Father is not in him. For all that is in the world, the lust of the FLESH [craving for sensual gratification], and the lust of the eyes [greedy longings of the MIND] and the PRIDE of life [assurance of one's own resources or in the stability of earthly things] - these do not come from the Father but are from the world. And the world passes away and disappears, and with it the forbidden craving [the passionate desires, the lust] of it; but he who does the will of God and carries out His purposes in his life, abides [remains] forever."* [AMP]

IN A NUTSHELL

1. Our true life is sustained from God's own mouth, breath [Spirit, initiative]

2. Don't be a trial to Him

3. Be dedicated. Become addicted to that intimate time of fellowship with Him, to obedience to what you hear Him say, and to seeing His smile of pleasure. Once we've seen His smile, baloney won't ever do again.

Chapter Three

BE ATTITUDES part two
The I AM Teaching Us TO BE
Matthew 4:17,19 & 5:1-12

*F*rom then on Jesus began to preach, "Repent of your sins and turn to God, for the Kingdom of Heaven is near." [this might say "Repent from your sins..." as in turn and run!] *Jesus called out to them, "Come, follow me, and I will show you how to fish for people!"*

One day as he saw the crowds gathering, Jesus went up on the mountainside and sat down. His disciples gathered around him, and he began to teach them.

"God blesses those who are poor and realize their need for him,
for the Kingdom of Heaven is theirs. [notice: is present tense]
God blesses those who mourn,
for they will be comforted.
God blesses those who are humble,
for they will inherit the whole earth.
God blesses those who hunger and thirst for justice,
for they will be satisfied.
God blesses those who are merciful,
for they will be shown mercy.
God blesses those whose hearts are pure,
for they will see God.
God blesses those who work for peace,
for they will be called the children of God.
God blesses those who are persecuted for doing right,
for the Kingdom of Heaven is theirs.
God blesses you when people mock you and persecute you and lie about you and say all sorts of evil things against you because you are my followers. Be happy about it! Be very glad! For a great reward

awaits you in heaven. And remember, the ancient prophets were persecuted in the same way." (NLT)

Matthew 4:12 picks up where Jesus has overcome the devil's temptations. Jesus hears that John the Baptist has been arrested and withdraws into Galilee. The next red letters we find are in verse 17 revealing the simple but penetrating message: REPENT FOR THE KINGDOM OF HEAVEN IS AT HAND!

This is a message for all people. Jesus came so that the whole world would have access to salvation (see John 3:17), but His first priority was the lost sheep of Israel (see Matthew 15:22-28). So this message of repentance is for all mankind, but here it was focused like light from the sun reflected through a magnifying glass concentrating the fire-starting beam on the nation who were called, and will always be, "God's chosen people," because they bore Torah, the Word and interactions of God, into the new age.

This is the same message John the Baptist had been preaching. John is now in prison but the message continues. We see Jesus take immediate steps to ensure that the message will even get to us. The next words we hear Him say are (v19): *"Come after me and I will make you fishers of men!"* Upon hearing these words, Peter and Andrew left their fishing business and became His disciples, as did Zebedee's sons, James and John. This was the beginning of a motley band of 12, through whom all the world would hear the name, Yeshua, Jesus, Isa, Jesu. [Note: the J in Greek at that time was pronounced like the J in other languages, as a Y. Jesus=Yesus correlating with the Hebrew pronunciation, Yeshuah.]

As we enter into the teaching of Jesus we must recognize that what He is saying may be in the hearing of a multitude, but is specifically for His disciples, those who have determined to follow and obey Him. His primary focus was on teaching these men. Keeping that in mind, and that Jesus is the Teacher, we will be less likely to isolate what He says or does in the historical context of Scripture, from the eternal context of what the Word made flesh is saying to us right now. That is one of the major pitfalls of the human mind and has almost single-handedly been responsible for every cult that has flourished under the thin guise of being "based on the teachings of Jesus."

Also, be careful not to take the "nuggets" that Jesus says and isolate them from the whole passage or scene in which it takes place. We have been guilty of that in so many sermons and as a result have ignorantly taught things that Jesus would never have said. We seem to think He is absent-minded, as if He is teaching along and suddenly just changes the subject and talks about something totally disconnected from the context of His discourse.

Neither Jesus nor the Holy Spirit, in His inspiration of the Scriptures, is senile. Every jot, tittle, word, sentence and paragraph has been deliberately placed exactly where it is to teach us and to do the unseen, deep surgery in us by the sharp double-edged sword of the Spirit – the scalpel of God. This can only be completed as we begin to observe the whole counsel of God in the mind-renewing panorama of the *whole* Word of God!

Then, as Jesus directs His focused power of teaching on His disciples, we can become His target. Yes, we can be the receiver of ALL that He taught those disciples - if we are truly and completely His disciple too. Let's join the inner group of those He has called now. Matt 5:1-12: *Seeing the crowds, He went up on the mountain, and when He was seated, His disciples came to Him. Then He opened His mouth and taught them saying:*

"Blessed are the poor in spirit, for theirs is the kingdom of heaven! (see Matt 4:17, connected directly to a life of repentance)

"Blessed are those who mourn, for they shall be comforted! (see Isa 61, connected directly to a life of repentance)

"Blessed are the meek, for they shall inherit the earth! (see Ps 37, connected directly to a life of repentance)

"Blessed are those who hunger and thirst for righteousness, for they shall be completely satisfied! (see Isa 55, connected directly to a life of repentance)

"Blessed are the merciful, for they shall obtain mercy! (see Matt 7, connected directly to a life of repentance)

"Blessed are the pure in heart, for they shall see God! (see Ps 24, connected directly to a life of repentance)

"Blessed are the makers and maintainers of peace, for they shall be called the sons of God! (look like Dad!)

"Blessed are those who are persecuted for righteousness sake, for theirs is the kingdom of heaven! (completes the thought, connecting to

poor in spirit.)

He elaborates: *"Blessed are you when people revile you and persecute you and say all kinds of evil things against you falsely on My account. Be glad, rejoice, for your reward in heaven is great* (strong and intense)*, for in this same way people persecuted the prophets who were before you."* (see 2Chronicles 36:16)

This passage is what is popularly called the BEATITUDES and is the first part of the Sermon on the Mount, which is recorded in Matthew 5 through 7. The word that is translated "blessed" here means, spiritually prosperous with life-joy and satisfaction in God's favor and salvation, regardless of your outward conditions. This is all the product of a life abandoned, habitually turning and going to God. In other words, walking daily in renewed fellowship with God no matter what is going on around us.

This was an incredibly effective attention grabber, and still is. Jesus is assaulting every man's own perception of "the way things are." Experience in this world says, "The person who...

    • allows his inner emotions and sensitivities to show;

    • doesn't take charge and make things happen the way he sees them;

    • doesn't down deep, really want personal success enough to be merciless; that person deserves to be trampled." Jesus is shouting that the exact opposite is true. Be GLAD? When people hurt you? What?!

Remember the first red letters, "Let's put aside your way of thinking and do things MY way, so that we can get the job done." In chapter 5, He is continuing to arrest our attention by saying, "Things are not as they appear! You want to know reality? Listen and heed what I say and I will give you the true picture." This sermon is also a prime example to show that Jesus is not senile. When He says in verse 13, *"You are the salt,"* He was not changing the subject. The whole discourse is about one subject and its goal is single – to introduce fallen man to the absolutes of the Kingdom of God and show our relationship to it. At the core, Jesus is saying, "If we are truly God's children, we are part of His household and here's the way things are seen and done in this Family!"

BE ATTITUDES - HERE'S TRUE HAPPINESS!

"Happy, to be envied, and spiritually prosperous are:

    • the humble, those who rate themselves insignificant (is this in conflict with today's philosophy, or what?);

    • those who mourn any separation from God and shun

anything that would result in grieving Him;

   • the mild, patient and long-suffering;

   • those who are ravenous for and will militantly guard a harmonious relationship with God;

   • those who can forgive and show kindness, not just to those who are kind, but especially to those who hurt them;

   • those who have seen what they are at their core and allow every thought and intent to be purified by the Fire of God's presence;

   • those who bring reconciliation and peace wherever they are, instead of stirring up strife and quarrels;

   • those who are persecuted for being like Jesus, doing things the way He does them and saying things the way He says them;

   • US, when people say all kinds of horrible things about us FALSELY because we are like Jesus (make sure they are false). Be glad and rejoice, for your reward is:

   • comfort

   • complete satisfaction and fulfillment

   • seeing God!

   • the Kingdom of Heaven

Twice He specifically gives the Kingdom of Heaven as reward to:

   • those who are humble

   • those who are persecuted.

To be persecuted is part of the package of repentance and receiving the Kingdom. *"They will persecute you... they hate me so they will hate you."* When we change our citizenship from this world to our real Homeland, the Kingdom of Heaven, we are going to naturally do and say things that are crazy to the world. That difference is the very thing that makes us the *"salt"* of the earth (v13), a preserving and curing influence. It is that very difference that makes us the *"light"* of the world (v15), a vessel for the Light from the real world, the Kingdom of God, to shine through, expelling the darkness and exposing Reality. That difference may well get us killed, but it is the very thing that gives us true and eternal value. In verse 16, Jesus says, *"Let your light so shine before men that they may see your moral excellence and your praiseworthy, noble and good deeds, and RECOGNIZE, HONOR, PRAISE AND GLORIFY YOUR FATHER WHO IS IN HEAVEN!"* (AMPC)

Chapter Four

HOW DOES A NEW CREATURE ACT? part one
Matthew 5:13-16 & 6

"*You are the salt of the earth; but if the salt loses its flavor, how shall it be seasoned? It is good for nothing but to be thrown out and trampled underfoot by men. You are the light of the world. A city that is set on a hill cannot be hidden. Nor do they light a lamp and put it under a basket, but on a lampstand and it gives light to all in the house. Let your light so shine before men, that they may see your good works and glorify your Father in heaven.*" (NKJV)

"*Watch out! Don't do your good deeds publicly, to be admired by others, for you will lose the reward from your Father in heaven. When you give to someone in need, don't do as the hypocrites do — blowing trumpets in the synagogues and streets to call attention to their acts of charity! I tell you the truth, they have received all the reward they will ever get.*"

"*But when you give to someone in need, don't let your left hand know what your right hand is doing. Give your gifts in private, and your Father, who sees everything, will reward you.*"

"*When you pray, don't be like the hypocrites who love to pray publicly on street corners and in the synagogues where everyone can see them. I tell you the truth, that is all the reward they will ever get.*"

"*But when you pray, go away by yourself, shut the door behind you, and pray to your Father in private. Then your Father, who sees everything, will reward you.*"

"*When you pray, don't babble on and on as people of other religions do. They think their prayers are answered merely by repeating their words again and again. Don't be like them, for your Father knows exactly what you need even before you ask him!*"

"*Pray like this:*"

"*Our Father in heaven, may your name be kept holy. May your*"

Kingdom come soon. May your will be done on earth, as it is in heaven. Give us today the food we need, and forgive us our sins, as we have forgiven those who sin against us. And don't let us yield to temptation, but rescue us from the evil one.

"If you forgive those who sin against you, your heavenly Father will forgive you. But if you refuse to forgive others, your Father will not forgive your sins.

"And when you fast, don't make it obvious, as the hypocrites do, for they try to look miserable and disheveled so people will admire them for their fasting. I tell you the truth, that is the only reward they will ever get.

"But when you fast, comb your hair and wash your face. Then no one will notice that you are fasting, except your Father, who knows what you do in private. And your Father, who sees everything, will reward you.

"Don't store up treasures here on earth, where moths eat them and rust destroys them, and where thieves break in and steal. Store your treasures in heaven, where moths and rust cannot destroy, and thieves do not break in and steal. Wherever your treasure is, there the desires of your heart will also be.

"Your eye is a lamp that provides light for your body. When your eye is good, your whole body is filled with light. But when your eye is bad, your whole body is filled with darkness. And if the light you think you have is actually darkness, how deep that darkness is!

"No one can serve two masters. For you will hate one and love the other; you will be devoted to one and despise the other. You cannot serve both God and money.

"That is why I tell you not to worry about everyday life — whether you have enough food and drink, or enough clothes to wear. Isn't life more than food, and your body more than clothing? Look at the birds. They don't plant or harvest or store food in barns, for your heavenly Father feeds them. And aren't you far more valuable to him than they are? Can all your worries add a single moment to your life?

"And why worry about your clothing? Look at the lilies of the field and how they grow. They don't work or make their clothing, yet Solomon in all his glory was not dressed as beautifully as they are. And if God cares so wonderfully for wildflowers that are here today and thrown into the fire tomorrow, he will certainly care for you. Why do you have so little faith?

"So don't worry about these things, saying, 'What will we eat? What will we drink? What will we wear?' These things dominate the *thoughts of unbelievers, but your heavenly Father already knows all your needs. Seek the Kingdom of God above all else, and live righteously, and he will give you everything you need.*

"So don't worry about tomorrow, for tomorrow will bring its own worries. Today's trouble is enough for today." (NLT)

We are exploring the contrast of God's ways versus our ways. In chapter 6 we will see the contrast in Matt 5:17-32 as a foundation for breaking free from our perspective enough to actually see God's perspective. Jesus challenged us to move the 'SIN BARRIER' to our inner man, our heart, a prerequisite for seeing from His point of view. Here, we are considering the contrast of God's ways and our ways with a goal to see the practical application. In other words, to simply acknowledge that His ways are very different from ours opens the door to real insight into who He is. And that's a wonderful thing! But to actually exchange our thoughts and actions for His in everyday practice – that's the real goal!

"You are the salt of the earth; but if the salt loses its flavor, how shall it be seasoned? It is good for nothing but to be thrown out and trampled underfoot by men. You are the light of the world. A city that is set on a hill cannot be hidden. Nor do they light a lamp and put it under a basket, but on a lampstand and it gives light to all in the house. Let your light so shine before men, that they may see your good works and glorify your Father in heaven." (Matthew 5:13-16).

Jesus did not come to demonstrate the life of a super-human. He came to show us how a normal human acts. To find out who our Father is and that our Family still exists is good news! Even better news is that our Father has been calling for us and has made all the arrangements for our reunion with Him and the rest of the Family.

Our Family had been kidnapped in ancient times. You and I were born in captivity and the only culture we've known is our captor's. So an encounter with one of our real Family would seem strange and wonderful indeed! Jesus is that One, our big Brother who is King of all kings and Lord of all lords, for He is the human Son of our Heavenly Father, born to a human mother, the Seed of the Holy Spirit; so that we, the Family in captivity, can be born again of the Holy Spirit and be re-initiated into our real Family.

Once that happens, we discover the standard by which we are to measure our Family-likeness has already been laid out for us in our Savior's human life and words (*the Way, the Truth, the Life*). It is apparent that we can accept this good news to be true and profess verbally the "lordship of Jesus Christ" and never actually activate the exchange of our life for His. This is most unfortunate because the point has always been the "exchange" of the whole life, from the inside out, culminating with the proclamation of our out-loud actions and words.

May I paraphrase?

Jesus' life speaks to us, "Here's the way we, God's Family, talk and think and respond."

Jesus personally says, "Now there are many members of the Family that need to be rescued before your kidnappers are judged. So, what I want you to do is live your life the way our Family lives, here in this captive culture so that I can, through you, contact every estranged member of the Family. I know that's impossible for you since all you know is the life of your captors, so I and our Father will come and make our home in your heart. From that secret place inside you, We will direct all the operations of your everyday life, orchestrating it with the rest of the Family's lives. In the meantime you can rest in the confidence that We know what We are doing. That will free you to give your attention to your new priorities – getting better acquainted with Us and carrying out the simple tasks We put in your hands every day."

Jesus continues, "When I'm living there in you, don't expect Me to even entertain thoughts that would lead you to do something I would not do. You won't murder anyone because I will not hold on to hard feelings or vindictive thoughts toward anyone. You won't fall into some sensual trap because I will never look at another human being as an object to use to satisfy some appetite of My Body or Mind. You won't lie because I know what is and what isn't, and I will help you rest in that. So if it's "yes" or if it's "no," you can just say it like it is. Your life won't be complicated by defense systems, insurance against loss, theft and abuse because now, through you, I'll be able to love and bless even the most abusive adversary. That's just the way we are."

"Furthermore, when we reach out and help someone, we don't do it so everyone will see and pat us on the back. When we pray, it's a private, one-on-One conversation with Dad. And when we talk to Him, that's where we do our forgiving and forgetting. When we fast, only Dad knows. Our stuff is all at our eternal address, Dad's House. We don't worry about material provision because our focus is single. We serve one Master, and we're living each moment to the max with Him."

Chapter Five

HOW DOES A NEW CREATURE ACT? part two
Matthew 7:1-14

"*D*o *not judge others, and you will not be judged. For you will be treated as you treat others. The standard you use in judging is the standard by which you will be judged.*

"*And why worry about a speck in your friend's eye when you have a log in your own? How can you think of saying to your friend, 'Let me help you get rid of that speck in your eye,' when you can't see past the log in your own eye? Hypocrite! First get rid of the log in your own eye; then you will see well enough to deal with the speck in your friend's eye.*

"*Don't waste what is holy on people who are unholy. Don't throw your pearls to pigs! They will trample the pearls, then turn and attack you.*

"*Keep on asking, and you will receive what you ask for. Keep on seeking, and you will find. Keep on knocking, and the door will be opened to you. For everyone who asks, receives. Everyone who seeks will find. And to everyone who knocks, the door will be opened.*

"*You parents—if your children ask for a loaf of bread, do you give them a stone instead? Or if they ask for a fish, do you give them a snake? Of course not! So if you sinful people know how to give good gifts to your children, how much more will your heavenly Father give good gifts to those who ask him.*

"*Do to others whatever you would like them to do to you. This is the essence of all that is taught in the law and the prophets.*

"*You can enter God's Kingdom only through the narrow gate. The highway to hell is broad, and its gate is wide for the many who choose that way. But the gateway to life is very narrow and the road is difficult, and only a few ever find it.*" (NLT)

Jesus instructs me to resist judging, condemning or trying

to fix others, at least until I get the beam out of my own eye. Here I am, with this big beam sticking out of the front of my head while trying to get close enough to some poor guy's face to do surgery on his eye? After all, the splinter may have even come from my beam! This is not about comparison. ["Well, you're surely the one to speak! You're the one that..."] The fact is, we recognize the fault we see in someone else because we are so intimately familiar with it. How easily we choose to either enforce or ignore the command "don't," based on whether or not the perceived need for correction seems urgent enough to risk retaliation. In other words, as we judge someone, we see ourselves as the self-sacrificing one, piously enduring the personal inconvenience. Thus, the person we love the most is the one we hurt the deepest. What an embarrassing picture of our relationships. And considering the nature of our hearts, changing that picture looks pretty hopeless. But there is good news! When God takes time to expose the darkness in our hearts, His purpose is not to BUM US OUT, but to BUST US OUT!

We sing, "He is our peace, who has broken down every wall." Ephesians 2:14 actually says He has "destroyed the hostile dividing wall between us" [AMP]. The walls between people are only too obvious. The point is that if this scripture is true, those walls DO NOT ACTUALLY EXIST any longer! The barriers between races and cultures, that have soaked our cities in blood, DO NOT EXIST! The walls that keep us from being really open, truthful and caring even to our own families, ARE NOT REALLY THERE! That is the "*IT*" in "*IT IS FINISHED!*"

Immediately, after Jesus made that announcement, Someone very tall and very strong walked into the temple and ripped the thick veil that separated the Holy from the Most Holy, from the top to the bottom like a paper napkin! In one moment, the pivotal moment of all time, He pulled down all that separates. Nothing has the power to separate us from our Father or our Family anymore. **Now,** with that Truth in mind, we would have to be in a hypnotic trance to go through our whole lives behind walls that are imaginary. We hold onto the muscle memory that keeps the illusion alive; the delusion of being superior, which is much easier from behind an imaginary wall. Step back and look at the big picture. Someone is taking advantage of our adolescent weaknesses, convincing us that those walls are real. Someone is messing with our minds! I wonder who that could be? Deception is one of only two powers that particular "someone" possesses.

Helped by our own fleshly pride, the deceiver *isolates* us behind imaginary walls. His other tool is *accusation*. From behind our walls we begin to hear his "insights" about our wife, husband, mother, father, in-laws, friend, pastor, employer, etc. Because we imagine ourselves separate from that person and look down from above their flaws, we agree with and begin to even voice those insights. For obvious reasons, this disorder plagues Christians more than any other people. Somewhere along the line, someone told us that we have a license to be "fruit inspectors." The scripture we quote is Matthew 7:15-16. Look at it. Does it say "Distrust and analyze everyone?" It doesn't even say, "Watch out for prophets." It says "Beware of *false* prophets." This is a test for suspected false prophets - not a test to put everybody we know through. Jesus' all-encompassing command in regards to relationship is: *LOVE ONE ANOTHER*. Pray for each other and give them room to grow out of the old nature and be formed into the new one, just as Jesus does toward us.

If we have the Holy Spirit dwelling in us like we say, there is a noticeable connection to what Jesus is actually doing and saying, RIGHT? Where is Jesus? What is He saying and doing right now? Psalm 110:1, Mark 16:19 and Hebrews 8:1 say that He is "seated at the right hand of the Father". Hebrews 7:25 says He is "constantly making petition to God, interceding with Him and intervening for those who come to God through Him." He is not just praying for us. He is fervently praying for that person who is the continual target of our criticism. Selah! (That means, "There! Whataya think about *that*?") He is defending them in the face of each of those accusations, which we hear in our minds and think it's because we're so discerning. We must choose the side we want to be on. Instead of agreeing with the accuser, we can join in with what Jesus is doing. That is why the Holy Spirit was given to us, so we can have the power to resist doing what our old twisted nature has always done, and do what Jesus is doing!

Here in Matthew 7:7-14, Jesus describes this intercession. "Ask and keep on asking until it is given. Seek and keep on seeking until it is found. Knock and keep knocking until the door opens." That is another passage that has been twisted by the prophets of self-worship religions. This is the practical how-to instruction for what to do when we see faults in a person. And, believe me, that person won't think nearly as much of our pearls of "insight" as we do, so don't try to fix people. Oswald Chambers calls that, being a "amateur Providence." Jesus is the only One who can do that. And if we'll get in on what He's doing, we'll find He was already working on it. We don't have to figure out what He WOULD do [*WWJD*]. There's no use in beating around the bush. Just BE WITH HIM. Boldly enter His prayer closet and join in with what He is already doing.

Think about what would happen if we looked at others through Jesus' eyes. What if we really began to feel what He feels toward them? Don't expect that to come natural in this life, but ask for the Holy Spirit's help not to react to things so quickly. Let Jesus come through and lead. Practice. Be patient. And remember this: No one can tell us what Jesus thinks but Him. Read His word, get up next to Him and listen. No counselor, no book or therapy can take the place of the knowing, submissive fellowship Jesus offers. This gate is narrow. But this is the gate we must enter. Jesus' way is love; love that is not just sympathy that can be patted on the back and tax-deductible. His love is self-sacrifice. Few even find this gate. Most of that is because we aren't even looking for it. So, even fewer actually go through it. Jesus did. To know and follow Him, that's Eternal Life!

Chapter Six

MOVING THE SIN BARRIER
Matthew 5:17-32

"Don't misunderstand why I have come. I did not come to abolish the law of Moses or the writings of the prophets. No, I came to accomplish their purpose. I tell you the truth, until heaven and earth disappear, not even the smallest detail of God's law will disappear until its purpose is achieved. So if you ignore the least commandment and teach others to do the same, you will be called the least in the Kingdom of Heaven. But anyone who obeys God's laws and teaches them will be called great in the Kingdom of Heaven.

"But I warn you—unless your righteousness is better than the righteousness of the teachers of religious law and the Pharisees, you will never enter the Kingdom of Heaven!

"You have heard that our ancestors were told, 'You must not murder. If you commit murder, you are subject to judgment.' But I say, if you are even angry with someone, you are subject to judgment! If you call someone an idiot, you are in danger of being brought before the court. And if you curse someone, you are in danger of the fires of hell.

"So if you are presenting a sacrifice at the altar in the Temple and you suddenly remember that someone has something against you, leave your sacrifice there at the altar. Go and be reconciled to that person. Then come and offer your sacrifice to God.

"When you are on the way to court with your adversary, settle your differences quickly. Otherwise, your accuser may hand you over to the judge, who will hand you over to an officer, and you will be thrown into prison. And if that happens, you surely won't be free again until you have paid the last penny.

"You have heard the commandment that says, 'You must not commit adultery.' But I say, anyone who even looks at a woman with lust has already committed adultery with her in his heart. So if your

25

eye—even your good eye—causes you to lust, gouge it out and throw it away. It is better for you to lose one part of your body than for your whole body to be thrown into hell. And if your hand—even your stronger hand—causes you to sin, cut it off and throw it away. It is better for you to lose one part of your body than for your whole body to be thrown into hell.

"You have heard the law that says, 'A man can divorce his wife by merely giving her a written notice of divorce.' But I say that a man who divorces his wife, unless she has been unfaithful, causes her to commit adultery. And anyone who marries a divorced woman also commits adultery. (NLT)

In the whole "Sermon on the Mount" Jesus is teaching us the basis for Real Life, life as a member of God's Family; how we think; how we act, and how we respond, as a person with Jesus' nature in authority over our inbred carnal nature. The "BEATITUDES" are a prime example of how drastically different God's ways are from ours.

"My thoughts are not your thoughts, neither are your ways My ways, says the Lord; For as the heavens are higher than the earth, so are My ways higher than your ways and My thoughts than your thoughts" (Isaiah 55:8-9).

"For we have all become like one who is unclean [ceremonially, like a leper], and all our righteousness (our best deeds of rightness and justice) is like filthy rags or a polluted garment; we all fade like a leaf, and our iniquities, like the wind, take us away [far from God's favor, hurrying us toward destruction]. And no one calls on Your name and awakens and bestirs himself to take and keep hold of You; for You have hidden Your face from us and have delivered us into the [consuming] power of our iniquities. YET, O LORD, YOU ARE OUR FATHER; we are the clay, and You our Potter, and we all are the work of Your hand" (Isaiah 64:6-8). His Hand... His Son... *"And the Word became flesh and lived awhile among us"* (John 1:14). We can actually feel the Potter's strong hand putting pressure on our lives to reshape us after His own pattern as *"the Word made flesh"* speaks!

We are to be the Light of the World. But it becomes painfully clear that the light is His, not ours. The only way we can be of value to the world around us is to have exchanged what we are, for what He is; to be possessed by Him, so that all the world sees is Jesus and the pure light of His personality, His wisdom, His reactions, in a surrendered human body – His word made flesh!

In verse 17 Jesus makes clear that even though what He is teaching seems new, He has come to simply finish everything that had been started. History is actually His-Story. All of history, the Law and the Prophets, were preparing mankind to hear and see the final page of God's redemptive plan. And right before their eyes, that promised fulfillment was a living reality. But there's a problem. God's people are in such a corrupt state of mind and spirit, they wouldn't recognize the Promise if it bit them on the nose. Which is pretty much what Jesus did on several occasions (v. 20). I pray that our continued study will accomplish that effect on us too. It should bite and shatter earthly perceptions – even of our Christianity – and fill us with His Reality.

Jesus confirms the absolute authority of the Law of God, the Law which they were so loyal to, or so they thought. Then He picks two points of that Law, murder and adultery, and proceeds to use those as examples to expose what the Law is really all about, contrasting their perception with His. He IS the Truth.

"You have heard that it was said to the men of old, You shall not kill, and whoever kills shall be liable to and unable to escape the punishment imposed by the court. But I say to you that everyone who continues to be angry with his brother or harbors malice (enmity of heart) against him shall be liable to and unable to escape the punishment imposed by the Sanhedrin, and whoever says, You cursed fool! [You empty-headed idiot!] shall be liable to and unable to escape the hell of fire" (v21-22 AMP).

We'll come back to what our subsequent actions should be later. Right now let's jump down to verse 27 and get His interpretation regarding adultery.

"You have heard that it was said, you shall not commit adultery. But I say to you that everyone who so much as looks at a woman with evil desire for her has already committed adultery with her in his heart."

We can see that until this moment these people perceived the Law as God's rules about man's physical actions. Jesus is saying, "That's not where the 'sin barrier' belongs. A sin barrier set up on the physical surface will not deal with the real sin. The Law did indeed accomplish something miraculous – the creation of the sin barrier. But that isn't enough. The next step is to MOVE THE SIN BARRIER INSIDE, from the place where bitterness or lust hatches and the deed is physically done, to the place where it is planted and takes root – the heart."

The effect of those words was, and is, explosive. I can just picture those guys as they reacted. It must have been something like, "You have to be kidding me!" From our own nature's perspective, that makes the Law not only very hard to live by, it makes it impossible! And that's the point. Beginning to see that it is impossible to please God by our own design, is the very thing that will drive us like a hurricane upon the Rock of His Grace. Shipwrecked and helpless, we will desperately cry out to God our Father, understanding that saving us is His work alone.

He who looks upon the hearts of men and women has proven beyond any doubt His motive and intent regarding His prize creation. He wants a level of intimacy with us that can only be experienced in the secrecy and privacy of the heart. On the cross He bought and paid for that piece of property because that's the headwaters of all the issues of our lives (Prov 4:23, Matt 15:18-19, Luke 6:45 – "*out of the heart*"). The heart is what He was always coming for. We stand in a generation that can look back over the patient and loving steps He has taken through His-Story. We can actually read the simple message written across time in the rise and fall of nations and across the universe in the beauty and awesomeness of His creation, "It's Me! Your Dad! I miss you! Please come Home!"

We are invited to move the sin barrier from our physical hands and lips to our heart. We will have a much more practical perspective on Who actually lives the life that pleases our Father. There's only One who can. He did it. He wants to do it again – in us. Let the way Jesus thinks, acts and responds become the way we think, act and respond. It's not enough to just try to be better or more self-disciplined. We have a part to play, but we must understand it is Him who wants to live His life in us. Our part is to persistently push aside our way and let Him.

Here's our part:

1. INVITE HIM IN AND LISTEN! This is not just a one-time deal. Invite Him into every situation, every circumstance, every day, every thought, every desire, every question, every pain. See what I mean? It's the full-time job of the believer. That's the "all your heart, mind, soul and strength" with which we are to love God. That simply means we will be addicted to reading His Book, spending time with Him and allowing the Holy Spirit to make us like Him, in our skin, to those around us.

2. PRACTICE! Our heart, mind, soul and strength are not easy to re-train. We must begin to catch ourselves in mid-stream and replace what we are about to say, with what He wants to say. Make an actual exchange between what we would normally do and what Jesus wants to do. Then we work with all the determination seen in verses 23-26

and 29-32. With the help of the Holy Spirit, we'll get the response time down, and let our emotional, mental and physical forces know Who's Boss... in every case. Our work is to practice until our disposition takes a backseat to His! Say what we hear Him say, do what we see Him do. Sound familiar?

This is a good place to read: Matthew 22:37, Luke 10:27, Deuteronomy 6:5, 29:29-30:20

Chapter Seven

BEWARE
Matthew 7:15-27

" *B*eware of false prophets, who come to you in sheep's cloth-ing, but inwardly they are ravenous wolves. You will know them by their fruits. Do men gather grapes from thorn-bushes, or figs from thistles? Even so, every good tree bears good fruit. A good tree cannot bear bad fruit, nor can a bad tree bear good fruit. Every tree that does not bear good fruit is cut down and thrown into the fire. Therefore by their fruits you will know them. Not everyone who says to me, 'Lord, Lord,' shall enter the kingdom of heaven, but he who does the will of my Father in heaven. Many will say to Me in that day, 'Lord, Lord, have we not prophesied in Your name, cast out demons in Your name, and done many wonders in Your name?' And then I will declare to them, I never knew you; depart from Me, you who practice lawlessness!"*

"Therefore whoever hears these sayings of mine, and does them, I will liken him to a wise man who built his house on the rock: and the rain descended, floods came, and the winds blew and beat on that house, and it did not fall, for it was founded on the rock. Now everyone who hears these sayings of Mine, and does not do them, will be like a foolish man who built his house on the sand and: the rain descended, the floods came, and the winds blew and beat on that house; and it fell. And great was its fall." (NKJV)

The simple message here is that the truth is very obvious if we will only pay attention. The fruit of ministry hangs out where all can see. We don't have to be deceived. Jesus is not talking about young plants here. He is talking about fruit bearing trees. We must be very caring and tolerant toward the young. The point is that if there is fruit being produced, then all we must do is observe the fruit and be able to distinguish real or unreal, bad or good.

It would be good at this point to ask the question, what is FRUIT? What are we looking at? When we look at highly visible ministries, is what we see the fruit? Well, when we think of media images we know that what we see is very enhanced and sometimes even manipulated. It may look real but it is not. It's only an image. Our first impressions of people even in person can be totally off. So the surface impressions and immediate conclusions we are led to make can be illusions. That may be *PART* of the FRUIT but couldn't possibly be *THE* FRUIT.

So, when Jesus says, *"By their fruits you will know them,"* He is challenging us to take an honest, intelligent look at the results. And that may not be right on the surface but should be apparent to any who will take a little closer look. Are the results real or just talk, and is what's being said what Jesus says? See, we don't have to wait and see if the thing will stand the test of time. We can know right now. It's either saying what Jesus says and doing what Jesus is doing, or it's not.

If we don't know what Jesus is saying or doing we'll buy into just about anything. That's the bottom line... KNOWING HIM. That's eternal life. Eternal life is not about the theatrics pulled off in His name. *"Not everyone who says 'Lord, Lord...' but he who does the will of My Father... Many will say, 'Haven't I [profited, oops! I mean] prophesied, cast out demons and done many wonders in Your Name?' And I will say to them, I never knew you. Get out of my sight."*

Can you imagine standing before Jesus and hearing those words? We are invited to build our life and ministry – our representation of God and His Kingdom – on the Rock. What and Who that Rock is, cannot be debated. It is clear. *"Therefore whoever hears these sayings of <u>mine</u> and does them..."*

CHECK IT OUT...

Are you a member of or an investor in a ministry that makes you wonder sometimes, "Is this the way Jesus does things?" Do you feel that kind of question would be considered out of order? Then STOP, pick up your Bible and read through all the red letters. Then read through them again. Then read how Jesus' disciples lived out what He had taught them. We don't have to be deceived! We can be sure we are following Jesus because we are getting to know Him better every day! We don't have to guess. God is the Judge, in the volume of the Book.

Chapter Eight

TO THE LEPER, THE CENTURION & THE RICH MAN
Matthew 8 & 9 (NKJV)

Jesus has been teaching us verbally. Now He teaches us by action. He touches people, illustrating how the reality of His kingdom and principles look when interpreted into action and relationships with the natural realities in people's lives. The first stage was the classroom. Now He goes into the field, the lab, to illustrate how it looks when this Love from the Father actually flows through a willing vessel.

The sequence of people He touches starts with the total outcast from society, then the strong self-sufficient and powerful man's-man. The list includes the current religious leaders, both legislative and spiritual, such as they were. The helpless, the hopeless, the abused, the opportunists and the actors are all personally addressed. Then there are the would-be followers, the sincere seekers and His true followers. He even seems to turn to the "class" and use the example of the centurion's faith to give another little nugget of truth. That seems to be a pretty complete sampling of the human varieties. Oh, He also spoke to demons. Hmm!

To the outcast, the leper - *"I am willing; be cleansed. See that you tell no one; but go your way, show yourself to the priest, and offer the gift that Moses commanded."*

To the man's-man, the centurion - *"I will come and heal him."*

To the "class", the people - *"Assuredly, I say to you, I have not found such great faith, not even in Israel! And I say to you that many will come from east and west, sit down with Abraham, Isaac, and Jacob in the kingdom of heaven. But the sons of the kingdom will be cast out into outer darkness. There will be weeping and gnashing of teeth."*

To the centurion - *"Go your way; and as you have believed, so let it be done for you."*

To the religious would-be followers, the scribe - *"Foxes* have holes and birds of the air have nests, but the Son of Man has nowhere to lay His head."

To His disciples - *"Why are you fearful, O you of little faith?"*

To demons - *"Go."*

To the helpless paralytic - *"Son, be of good cheer; your sins are forgiven you."*

To the law-givers, the scribes - *"Why do you think evil in your hearts? For which is easier, to say, 'Your sins are forgiven you,' or to say, 'Arise and walk'? But that you may know that the Son of Man has power on earth to forgive sins..."*

To the helpless paralytic - *"Arise, take up your bed, and go to your house."*

To the opportunist, the tax collector, Matthew - *"Follow me."*

To the religious Pharisees - *"Those who are well have no need of a physician, but those who are sick. But go and learn what this means: I desire mercy and not sacrifice. For I did not come to call the righteous, but sinners, to repentance."*

To committed seekers, John's disciples - *"Can the friends of the bridegroom mourn as long as the bridegroom is with them? But the days will come when the bridegroom will be taken away from them, and then they will fast. No one puts a piece of un-shrunk cloth on an old garment; for the patch pulls away from the garment, and the tear is made worse. Nor do people put new wine into old wineskins, or else the wineskins break, the wine is spilled, and the wineskins are ruined. But they put new wine into new wineskins, and both are preserved."*

To the abused woman - *"Be of good cheer, daughter; your faith has made you well."*

To the actors, the mourners - *"Make room, for the girl is not dead, but sleeping."*

To the hopeless blind man - *"Do you believe that I am able to do this? According to your faith let it be to you. See that no one knows it."*

To His disciples - *"The harvest is plentiful, but the laborers are few. Therefore pray the Lord of the harvest to send more laborers into His harvest."*

Jesus is willing. We don't have to talk Him into saving us or healing us or restoring us. He is willing to come to us where we are and take care of what needs to be done. Jesus was here for a specific purpose: to show us how our Father feels toward us. *"God so loved the world that He..."*

He is willing. In fact He's the one who is actually seeking us. And there's more good news: If we have turned to Him and let Him move into our heart, He has begun a good work in us and He is going to finish it.

Now that's the best news you will hear all day! He said it, I believe it and THAT'S *THAT*!

Chapter Nine

INSTRUCTIONS TO APPRENTICES
Matthew 10:5-42

*J*esus sent out the twelve apostles with these instructions: "Don't go to the Gentiles or the Samaritans, but only to the people of Israel—God's lost sheep. Go and announce to them that the Kingdom of Heaven is near. Heal the sick, raise the dead, cure those with leprosy, and cast out demons. Give as freely as you have received!*

"Don't take any money in your money belts—no gold, silver, or even copper coins. Don't carry a traveler's bag with a change of clothes and sandals or even a walking stick. Don't hesitate to accept hospitality, because those who work deserve to be fed.

"Whenever you enter a city or village, search for a worthy person and stay in his home until you leave town. When you enter the home, give it your blessing. If it turns out to be a worthy home, let your blessing stand; if it is not, take back the blessing. If any household or town refuses to welcome you or listen to your message, shake its dust from your feet as you leave. I tell you the truth, the wicked cities of Sodom and Gomorrah will be better off than such a town on the judgment day.

"Look, I am sending you out as sheep among wolves. So be as shrewd as snakes and harmless as doves. But beware! For you will be handed over to the courts and will be flogged with whips in the synagogues. You will stand trial before governors and kings because you are my followers. But this will be your opportunity to tell the rulers and other unbelievers about me. When you are arrested, don't worry about how to respond or what to say. God will give you the right words at the right time. For it is not you who will be speaking—it will be the Spirit of your Father speaking through you.

"A brother will betray his brother to death, a father will betray his own child, and children will rebel against their parents and cause them to be killed. And all nations will hate you because you are my

followers. But everyone who endures to the end will be saved. When you are persecuted in one town, flee to the next. I tell you the truth, the Son of Man will return before you have reached all the towns of Israel.

"Students are not greater than their teacher, and slaves are not greater than their master. Students are to be like their teacher, and slaves are to be like their master. And since I, the master of the household, have been called the prince of demons, the members of my household will be called by even worse names!

"But don't be afraid of those who threaten you. For the time is coming when everything that is covered will be revealed, and all that is secret will be made known to all. What I tell you now in the darkness, shout abroad when daybreak comes. What I whisper in your ear, shout from the housetops for all to hear!

"Don't be afraid of those who want to kill your body; they cannot touch your soul. Fear only God, who can destroy both soul and body in hell. What is the price of two sparrows—one copper coin? But not a single sparrow can fall to the ground without your Father knowing it. And the very hairs on your head are all numbered. So don't be afraid; you are more valuable to God than a whole flock of sparrows.

"Everyone who acknowledges me publicly here on earth, I will also acknowledge before my Father in heaven. But everyone who denies me here on earth, I will also deny before my Father in heaven.

"Don't imagine that I came to bring peace to the earth! I came not to bring peace, but a sword. 'I have come to set a man against his father, a daughter against her mother, and a daughter-in-law against her mother-in-law. Your enemies will be right in your own household!'

"If you love your father or mother more than you love me, you are not worthy of being mine; or if you love your son or daughter more than me, you are not worthy of being mine. If you refuse to take up your cross and follow me, you are not worthy of being mine. If you cling to your life, you will lose it; but if you give up your life for me, you will find it.

"Anyone who receives you receives me, and anyone who receives me receives the Father who sent me. If you receive a prophet as one who speaks for God, you will be given the same reward as a prophet. And if you receive righteous people because of their righteousness, you will be given a reward like theirs. And if you give even a cup of cold water to one of the least of my followers, you will surely be rewarded." (NLT)

Jesus called His disciples around Him and gave them authority to cast out unclean spirits and heal sickness and disease. They were Peter and Andrew, James and John, Phillip and Bartholomew [Nathaniel], Thomas and Matthew, James and Thaddaeus [Judas, not Iscariot], Simon and Judas, who betrayed Him. Jesus was sending these 12 out on their first ministry tour, so He gave them these instructions:

"Don't go to the Gentiles or the Samaritans. Go only to the Jews. Preach this message: THE REALITY AND SUBSTANCE OF GOD IS NOW IN REACH! Heal the sick, cleanse the lepers, raise the dead, cast out demons. Pour out freely what you have freely received. Don't take money or baggage or extra provisions for the journey. You will eat what you are given as a sojourning laborer."

The beginnings of service are always meager. But that isn't only because, as in the business world, you start out small and work your way up. Making parallels between business and ministry seems to be a very common mistake lately and has caused many problems in the Church. The beginnings are meager for a very specific purpose: to establish dependency upon God.

That is a great irony. Jesus loads these human vessels up with priceless gifts and they don't even have the price of a donut. As they carried out His specific instructions they were totally dependent for their basic daily needs on the people they were distributing those gifts to. That could be very humbling. That means it would be very difficult for them to use this "giftedness" for personal gain. One more little thing it means – they needed to be nice.

Now, if you know that this was not the only trip Jesus sent them on, you also surely agree that this scene is not there to cause us to take a "vow of poverty". The point is that these men needed to establish the foundation stone of trusting-dependency in their relationship to God. It probably took a while to get free from the anxiety that comes from not knowing if you will have any dinner. But once that stone was firmly in place they were free to focus on and enjoy doing the work that Jesus had given them to do. When they returned, they were not testifying of how well they ate. They were excited about the result of the authority they had in Jesus' name. (Of course, that brought up the need for another little lesson, which will come in Luke 10:20.) The point is, they weren't caught up in planning and managing things so that their basic needs would be met. They were busy doing the specific job that they had been given.

Can we stop for a moment and ask the Lord to show us how this example can be applied to our present circumstances? Remember, don't think of anything Jesus says as words for someone else. Whatever He speaks, it's first directly to us, personally.

Chapter Ten

SHEEP & WOLVES, SERPENTS & DOVES
Matthew 10:16-42

"*L*ook, I am sending you out as sheep among wolves. So be as shrewd as snakes and harmless as doves. But beware! For you will be handed over to the courts and will be flogged with whips in the synagogues. You will stand trial before governors and kings because you are my followers. But this will be your opportunity to tell the rulers and other unbelievers about me. When you are arrested, don't worry about how to respond or what to say. God will give you the right words at the right time. For it is not you who will be speaking—it will be the Spirit of your Father speaking through you.*

"A brother will betray his brother to death, a father will betray his own child, and children will rebel against their parents and cause them to be killed. And all nations will hate you because you are my followers. But everyone who endures to the end will be saved. When you are persecuted in one town, flee to the next. I tell you the truth, the Son of Man will return before you have reached all the towns of Israel.

"Students are not greater than their teacher, and slaves are not greater than their master. Students are to be like their teacher, and slaves are to be like their master. And since I, the master of the household, have been called the prince of demons, the members of my household will be called by even worse names!

"But don't be afraid of those who threaten you. For the time is coming when everything that is covered will be revealed, and all that is secret will be made known to all. What I tell you now in the darkness, shout abroad when daybreak comes. What I whisper in your ear, shout from the housetops for all to hear!

"Don't be afraid of those who want to kill your body; they cannot touch your soul. Fear only God, who can destroy both soul and body in hell. What is the price of two sparrows—one copper coin? But not a single sparrow can fall to the ground without your Father knowing it.

And the very hairs on your head are all numbered. So don't be afraid; you are more valuable to God than a whole flock of sparrows.

"Everyone who acknowledges me publicly here on earth, I will also acknowledge before my Father in heaven. But everyone who denies me here on earth, I will also deny before my Father in heaven.

"Don't imagine that I came to bring peace to the earth! I came not to bring peace, but a sword.

'I have come to set a man against his father, a daughter against her mother, and a daughter-in-law against her mother-in-law. Your enemies will be right in your own household!'

"If you love your father or mother more than you love me, you are not worthy of being mine; or if you love your son or daughter more than me, you are not worthy of being mine. If you refuse to take up your cross and follow me, you are not worthy of being mine. If you cling to your life, you will lose it; but if you give up your life for me, you will find it.

"Anyone who receives you receives me, and anyone who receives me receives the Father who sent me. If you receive a prophet as one who speaks for God, you will be given the same reward as a prophet. And if you receive righteous people because of their righteousness, you will be given a reward like theirs. And if you give even a cup of cold water to one of the least of my followers, you will surely be rewarded." (NLT)

Jesus is speaking…(my paraphrase)

"Look, I'm sending you out like sheep into a pack of wolves, so be aware and quick like a snake but as guileless and innocent as a dove. Be on your guard for men who will report your actions as 'evil and criminal' to antagonistic religious leaders. They will even beat you right in their churches. You'll be arrested and brought to trial. But this will only confirm their final judgment. When you are brought to trial, don't think about what you are going to say. It will be given to you even as you speak. It won't be you speaking but your Father speaking in you."

"Don't be surprised when it is your own family members that turn you in. You'll be hated by everyone because of Me, but just keep going. When you are persecuted in one city, run to another. You will not get to all the cities of Israel before I come. What I say in our private conversations, preach it openly in public. Don't let their threats and slander paralyze you. They did the same to me so why would it be any different for you? They can only kill what will die anyway. So don't fear them, fear and obey God. You are very valuable to Him and

He will take good care of you. As long as you are speaking for Me, I am speaking for you to the Father. Don't let that communication be broken by fear of men."

"And don't think this turmoil means that I have lost control. This is the exact result My coming was meant to produce. It will truly expose those who really love and follow Me. The one who can not turn away from whatever is against Me is deceived, believing that he is saving himself. But it's really just the opposite. Only by letting go of what seems to be his life will he save his real life. So the ones that receive you, some at the risk of their reputations and freedom, are receiving Me. The reward for receiving you is that they receive the Life I give you."

At first glance, these words from Jesus to His disciples sound very appropriate for them and maybe for some of our missionary brothers who minister in hostile cultures, but not especially relevant to us. After all, it is still pretty popular in this country to be a Christian. Or, is it? There are people who adamantly say it is unconstitutional to teach or talk about biblical values in our public institutions, unless, of course, we agree that everybody goes to heaven. Then, of course, we can teach everything and anything we want to, as long as we are not "fundamentalist born-agains". Applied to followers of Jesus, that means we believe there's one God who wrote a Book and sent His Son so we could know Him and be with Him. That, to the Parliament of the World's Religions [started in 1893], is the greatest enemy to true peace and harmony in the world.

Once we consider these developments, we could actually read these words of Jesus and take them as a warning to us. One thing is made very clear for every reader – life is not what it seems. Reality is defined differently from two very different points of view. One point of view is ours. The other is God's, which can be ours if we choose to let Him overrule our natural way of seeing things. That's where we get the term super-natural. The natural is overcome by the super(natural). The dark is overcome by light; isolation, overcome by reconciliation; indifference, overcome by love; and death is overcome by life.

Perhaps the greatest evidence that there is a God is that we have this sense of contrast and struggle between dark and light, wrong and right. These self-filled, new age hybrid Hindu-"Christian" philosophers make a grave mistake in their logic when they attack us dangerous fundamentalists. They presume the only reason we have that guilt-producing sense of right and wrong is that we grew up under the brainwashing tactics of Bible-thumping Christians. By denying the existence of a Father/Creator/God, they miss the fact that He designed and initiated the whole thing, so He could have His family back. *"He seeks genuine worshippers," "... God so loved the world that He gave His only begotten Son, that whosoever believes..."* Guilt is one of the spiritual senses given to warn, so that we can shift to avoid danger. It is the soul's senses that alert us to the spiritual equivalent of sight to let us know the action called for if there is an on-coming train or a welcoming glance from our wife. It is also to the equivalent of touch that lets us feel the heat of fire or lush texture of fine leather; and of hearing that distinguishes between noise and music; and of smell that tells us we just stepped in something the dog left or there's steak on the barbie. Those spiritual senses are given so we can be aware of spiritual conditions around us and be able to respond appropriately.

Chapter Eleven

ARE YOU THE ONE?
Matthew 11

*W*hen Jesus had finished giving these instructions to his twelve disciples, he went out to teach and preach in towns throughout the region.

John the Baptist, who was in prison, heard about all the things the Messiah was doing. So he sent his disciples to ask Jesus, "Are you the Messiah we've been expecting, or should we keep looking for someone else?"

Jesus told them, "Go back to John and tell him what you have heard and seen—the blind see, the lame walk, the lepers are cured, the deaf hear, the dead are raised to life, and the Good News is being preached to the poor. And tell him, God blesses those who do not turn away because of me."

As John's disciples were leaving, Jesus began talking about him to the crowds. "What kind of man did you go into the wilderness to see? Was he a weak reed, swayed by every breath of wind? Or were you expecting to see a man dressed in expensive clothes? No, people with expensive clothes live in palaces. Were you looking for a prophet? Yes, and he is more than a prophet. John is the man to whom the Scriptures refer when they say, 'Look, I am sending my messenger ahead of you, and he will prepare your way before you.'

"I tell you the truth, of all who have ever lived, none is greater than John the Baptist. Yet even the least person in the Kingdom of Heaven is greater than he is! And from the time John the Baptist began preaching until now, the Kingdom of Heaven has been forcefully advancing, and violent people are attacking it. For before John came, all the prophets and the law of Moses looked forward to this present time. And if you are willing to accept what I say, he is Elijah, the one the prophets said would come. Anyone with ears to hear should listen and understand!

"To what can I compare this generation? It is like children playing a game in the public square. They complain to their friends,

'We played wedding songs,
and you didn't dance,
so we played funeral songs,
and you didn't mourn.'

"For John didn't spend his time eating and drinking, and you say, 'He's possessed by a demon.' The Son of Man, on the other hand, feasts and drinks, and you say, 'He's a glutton and a drunkard, and a friend of tax collectors and other sinners!' But wisdom is shown to be right by its results."

Jesus began to denounce the towns where he had done so many of his miracles, because they hadn't repented of their sins and turned to God. "What sorrow awaits you, Korazin and Bethsaida! For if the miracles I did in you had been done in wicked Tyre and Sidon, their people would have repented of their sins long ago, clothing themselves in burlap and throwing ashes on their heads to show their remorse. I tell you, Tyre and Sidon will be better off on judgment day than you.

"And you people of Capernaum, will you be honored in heaven? No, you will go down to the place of the dead. For if the miracles I did for you had been done in wicked Sodom, it would still be here today. I tell you, even Sodom will be better off on judgment day than you."

At that time Jesus prayed this prayer: "O Father, Lord of heaven and earth, thank you for hiding these things from those who think themselves wise and clever, and for revealing them to the childlike. Yes, Father, it pleased you to do it this way!

"My Father has entrusted everything to me. No one truly knows the Son except the Father, and no one truly knows the Father except the Son and those to whom the Son chooses to reveal him."

Then Jesus said, "Come to me, all of you who are weary and carry heavy burdens, and I will give you rest. Take my yoke upon you. Let me teach you, because I am humble and gentle at heart, and you will find rest for your souls. For my yoke is easy to bear, and the burden I give you is light." (NLT)

Jesus and John the Baptist were cousins, but their relationship is much more than familiar. A deep connection is once again illustrated (see Matt 3:13-15) in this expression, which seems to be a spontaneous pouring from Jesus' heart in response to communication from John the Baptist. He reconfirms John's purpose and real identity in the large picture of the establishment of God's Kingdom.

Hearing about the works that Jesus was doing may have been a signal in the timing of the events in God's plan. We don't know what John was going through in prison. We can make some educated guesses, but we can't really know what made him ask, *"Are you the One?"* It occurs to me that it could have been a final checkpoint to clear in making sure John had finished his God-given task... kind of a compulsory riddle that had only one answer. Getting the exact answer would release John and confirm that, *"YES! I am done!"*

I'm not sure that I agree with those who believe that John was confused or doubting. I <u>am</u> convinced that Jesus (absolutely) and John (very likely) were the only people, beside the Father, who really knew the timetable and what was happening at that moment. This marker indicated a fully engaged ministry for Jesus, but for John, it was the finish line. Jesus' words were the perfect answer to the question and came right out of the Manual (see Isaiah 35:5, 42:7, 61:1, Psalm 22:26). If this interpretation is even close, then verse 6 can't mean, "You better watch out, John. You better not be doubting me." It would have to be more like, "It's okay, dear cousin, you have carried out your commission. Go ahead, I'll see you in a few days." I can't think of a swifter way to speed through the finish line than the way John did it. If you can get past the gore, you can see that he blasted off this planet like a rocket.

Jesus then seals this marker in time with a little recap exposition honoring John. *"He was a real man, a real prophet and more. He's the one, the messenger"* (see Malachi 3:1). A secret comes out, just pops to the surface – a little bonus, *"If you will accept it - John is Elijah"* (see Malachi 4:5).

I know that God can do anything He wants, but you have to admit, that is a tough one to process! Then Jesus makes it sound like, if I've got ears, I should be able to hear that. Not only that, He unleashes an attack on the places that were on the deaf list. Whew! How hard of hearing are we? Just how spiritually blind and arrogant is this generation?

Jesus says (in my loose paraphrase), "It's like we (John and I) were calling to you [this generation] to come play and all you could do was find silly justifications for not playing with us. John isolated himself and followed the Law in Nazarite zeal and you said he was crazy. I went to your parties and feasts and you say I'm a drunk and a glutton who hangs out with the wrong crowd. But the proof will be very plain to see; and the proof is going to be pretty ugly for places like Chorazin, Bethsaida and Capernaum. You saw the mighty works, the very heart of

God poured out in behalf of your people but you did not repent! It will be more tolerable for Tyre, Sidon and Sodom on the day of judgment than for you! If they had seen what you've seen they would have repented long ago."

Jesus then looks into His Father's eyes and thanks Him for taking pleasure in hiding these truths from the *"wise and prudent"* and revealing them to babes. Then He looks into our eyes and says, "Everything has been handed over to me from my Father. He is the only one who knows me, His Son, and no one knows Him but me and those I choose to reveal Him to. So come to Me, all you who are tired and overwhelmed, and I'll give you rest. Accept my work as yours. Watch me and learn that my way is one of gentleness and humility; and you will be deeply and permanently refreshed. Because the weight of my work is distributed perfectly... fitted perfectly... and the task is easy."

Chapter Twelve

IS THE LORD RULER OF THE RULES?
Or
DO THE RULES RULE THE RULER?
Matthew 12:1-14

*A*t about that time Jesus was walking through some grain-fields on the Sabbath. His disciples were hungry, so they be-gan breaking off some heads of grain and eating them. But some Pharisees saw them do it and protested, "Look, your disciples are breaking the law by harvesting grain on the Sabbath."

Jesus said to them, "Haven't you read in the Scriptures what David did when he and his companions were hungry? He went into the house of God, and he and his companions broke the law by eating the sacred loaves of bread that only the priests are allowed to eat. And haven't you read in the law of Moses that the priests on duty in the Temple may work on the Sabbath? I tell you, there is one here who is even greater than the Temple! But you would not have condemned my innocent disciples if you knew the meaning of this Scripture: 'I want you to show mercy, not offer sacrifices.' For the Son of Man is Lord, even over the Sabbath!"

Then Jesus went over to their synagogue, where he noticed a man with a deformed hand. The Pharisees asked Jesus, "Does the law permit a person to work by healing on the Sabbath?" (They were hoping he would say yes, so they could bring charges against him.) And he answered, "If you had a sheep that fell into a well on the Sabbath, wouldn't you work to pull it out? Of course you would. And how much more valuable is a person than a sheep! Yes, the law permits a person to do good on the Sabbath."

Then he said to the man, "Hold out your hand." So the man held out his hand, and it was restored, just like the other one! Then the Pharisees called a meeting to plot how to kill Jesus. (NLT)

It is the Sabbath, the holy day. The sacred hours, from sundown Friday to sundown Saturday, during which the LAW was supreme boss. That LAW originated from the 10 commandments given to Moses by God on Mount Sinai. Of course, by the time Jesus is walking through this grain field that very complete list of demands had been interpreted and analyzed, expounded and expanded by the religious scholars and included volumes and volumes of rules and applications. Because the common man on the street could get nowhere close to knowing or even reading all those rules. There were always, it seems, the ever-present religious police: the Pharisees, Sadducees and scribes. These guys were on Jesus and His disciples constantly, looking for any little infraction. He was making it all too simple and available to every one. So they were gathering evidence against Him to protect their jobs as the keepers of the rules, which gave them an impressive and long-held power over the nation.

Jesus' disciples were crushing the grain in their hands and eating it. The police turned their siren on, pulled them over and wrote them up on a technical violation, for "harvesting" and "threshing" on the Sabbath. Jesus' answer was not meant to refute the law of the Sabbath but to show that the law was meant for the benefit of man and that the Boss of the rules and the King of the Kingdom was present. His reference back to David's use of the sacred show-bread to feed his men illustrated that God cares more about man being fed when he's hungry than He cares about the rules being followed. In fact the point of the Sabbath was that man would rest and be fed and regenerated.

So it was with the incident in the synagogue. They were watching to catch Jesus in a technical crime because they knew He would see the man with the withered hand. From Jesus' point of view, of course they should expect Him to heal the man, especially on the Sabbath. His illustration was perfect for them. They had flocks. After all, they were the richest men in the community. They obviously would not just allow one of their flock to stay lost or in a pit through a whole day. It would die.

So Jesus says in no uncertain terms, *The rules of God are meant for the welfare of man, not to bind or constrain.* Paul said, "So does that mean we are to take that as license to satisfy our every whim? Of course not" (see Rom 6:15). Inherent in the rules is the ultimate need to come to God. Where else can welfare and benefit be found in its fullest form?

Another way of looking at this issue is to recognize that God perceives rules differently than we do. We see rules as a line. On one side there is favor. On the other is discipline. A person is either on one side of the line or the other. The people on one side use the rules to "rule" over the people on the other. Much like the guards in a prison use the rules on the inmates. The police enforce rules on drivers. The corporate management rule the employees by the rules they set. With all these life examples it is hard to see rules like God sees them.

He sees the real rules as empowering and stabilizing installations for the benefit of people and the communion with people. He loves people. From our perception of rules, one of three things is always happening. Either we are blatantly violating the rules, bending them by hedging them or we are keeping them, which usually is taken to mean we are qualified to enforce them on others. So our view of God is "enforcer." But He has communicated guidelines so that we would ultimately be empowered to live the life of Christ, not by rules, but by love.

The "Law" was given to show us that without knowing God and allowing Him to supernaturally install His nature in us, it is impossible to meet the requirements. That discovery drives our ship onto the reef of His grace, where we find that all He ever wanted was to have us close to Him, residing with Him, depending on Him, getting to know Him better every day.

Once we are restored to the right relationship with Him, the rules have little value for we have reached the end to which they were the means. We no longer go to church because we are *supposed* to. We go because we want to fellowship with the Family around the Head of the Family. We no longer read the Bible just because we are supposed to. We read His Book because we want to learn more about Him. Now, it is His love that compels and constrains, not His rules.

Jesus says, "*If you had only understood what God meant when He said, 'I require mercy, rather than sacrifice,' you would not be condemning the innocent. For I am the RULER over the Sabbath.*"

Chapter Thirteen

WHO IS JESUS? & WHO IS HIS FAMILY?
Matthew 12:15ff

*B*ut *Jesus knew what they were planning. So he left that area, and many people followed him. He healed all the sick among them, but he warned them not to reveal who he was. This fulfilled the prophecy of Isaiah concerning him:*

> *"Look at my Servant, whom I have chosen.*
> *He is my Beloved, who pleases me.*
> *I will put my Spirit upon him, and he will proclaim justice to the nations.*
> *He will not fight or shout or raise his voice in public.*
> *He will not crush the weakest reed or put out a flickering candle.*
> *Finally he will cause justice to be victorious.*
> *And his name will be the hope of all the world."*

Then a demon-possessed man, who was blind and couldn't speak, was brought to Jesus. He healed the man so that he could both speak and see. The crowd was amazed and asked, "Could it be that Jesus is the Son of David, the Messiah?" But when the Pharisees heard about the miracle, they said, "No wonder he can cast out demons. He gets his power from Satan, the prince of demons."

Jesus knew their thoughts and replied, "Any kingdom divided by civil war is doomed. A town or family splintered by feuding will fall apart. And if Satan is casting out Satan, he is divided and fighting against himself. His own kingdom will not survive. And if I am empowered by Satan, what about your own exorcists? They cast out demons, too, so they will condemn you for what you have said. But if I am casting out demons by the Spirit of God, then the Kingdom of God has arrived among you. For who is powerful enough to enter the house of a strong man like Satan and plunder his goods? Only someone even stronger—someone who could tie him up and then plunder his house.

"Anyone who isn't with me opposes me, and anyone who isn't working with me is actually working against me.

"So I tell you, every sin and blasphemy can be forgiven—except blasphemy against the Holy Spirit, which will never be forgiven. Anyone who speaks against the Son of Man can be forgiven, but anyone who speaks against the Holy Spirit will never be forgiven, either in this world or in the world to come.

"A tree is identified by its fruit. If a tree is good, its fruit will be good. If a tree is bad, its fruit will be bad. You brood of snakes! How could evil men like you speak what is good and right? For whatever is in your heart determines what you say. A good person produces good things from the treasury of a good heart, and an evil person produces evil things from the treasury of an evil heart. And I tell you this, you must give an account on judgment day for every idle word you speak. The words you say will either acquit you or condemn you."

One day some teachers of religious law and Pharisees came to Jesus and said, "Teacher, we want you to show us a miraculous sign to prove your authority."

But Jesus replied, "Only an evil, adulterous generation would demand a miraculous sign; but the only sign I will give them is the sign of the prophet Jonah. For as Jonah was in the belly of the great fish for three days and three nights, so will the Son of Man be in the heart of the earth for three days and three nights.

"The people of Nineveh will stand up against this generation on judgment day and condemn it, for they repented of their sins at the preaching of Jonah. Now someone greater than Jonah is here—but you refuse to repent. The queen of Sheba will also stand up against this generation on judgment day and condemn it, for she came from a distant land to hear the wisdom of Solomon. Now someone greater than Solomon is here—but you refuse to listen.

"When an evil spirit leaves a person, it goes into the desert, seeking rest but finding none. Then it says, 'I will return to the person I came from.' So it returns and finds its former home empty, swept, and in order. Then the spirit finds seven other spirits more evil than itself, and they all enter the person and live there. And so that person is worse off than before. That will be the experience of this evil generation."

As Jesus was speaking to the crowd, his mother and brothers stood outside, asking to speak to him. Someone told Jesus, "Your mother and your brothers are outside, and they want to speak to you."

Jesus asked, "Who is my mother? Who are my brothers?" Then he pointed to his disciples and said, "Look, these are my mother and brothers. Anyone who does the will of my Father in heaven is my brother and sister and mother!" (NLT)

This seems to be a little bigger bite of scripture to take at once but there are a couple of clarifications here that are related. The first is clarifying **WHO JESUS IS** and the second clarifies **WHO JESUS' FAMILY IS**.

The first thing we can note is Jesus' response to what was happening in verse 14. When He saw that the council was meeting to devise some way to do away with Him, He left from there. He also told the people who were healed not to tell anyone. Then it seems like Matt takes a left turn when he tells us why Jesus does that. He says that it is to fulfill a prophecy by Isaiah, which he quotes directly from Isaiah 42:1-4, giving us insight into what descriptions such as breaking a bruised reed, quenching smoking flax and crying out in the streets are talking about. Most importantly though, this gives us insight into the person of Jesus. Therein is found the overarching objective of these words and events (and yes, God's whole Book).

WHO IS JESUS?

First He does something that is described by Isaiah: He left town and told His people not to talk. Then some of the same proof of identity that Jesus had sent back to John the Baptist (also in Isaiah 29, 42 and Psalm 146) becomes a living illustration in verse 22 in the person of the blind and dumb demoniac. Immediately, the amazed people say, "Wow! Doesn't this prove He's the Messiah?" Of course the politicians wouldn't take that lying down, blindly stumbling into Jesus' trap-for-fools. They countered with what seems to be a hasty accusation that Jesus drove the demons out by the power of the prince of demons, Beelzebub. This reaction only has its full meaning if you see that this blind, dumb, possessed man was also an illustration of the actual spiritual condition of those religious leaders. They were infected, and by them the infection had spread throughout the whole nation (see Rev 3:17). As quickly as He dispatched the demons themselves, Jesus put the politicians in their place and gave even further support to the people's conclusion that He was the Messiah.

WHO IS JESUS' FAMILY?

Jesus turns on the bedrock of His own identity to point out His true followers, His true Family. The key words are *"with me...Those who are not with me... He that gathers not with me..."* This defined both those that are His and those that are not.

Then another major left turn! Jesus continues with, *"That's why I say to you, all kinds of sin, even blasphemy shall be forgiven, except for that against the Holy Spirit. You can talk against Me and it will be forgiven, but if you talk against the Holy Spirit it will never be forgiven."*

What does that have to do with being *"with Him"*? He is using this *"generation of vipers"* whose mouths reveal the abundance of evil in their hearts, to illustrate what it is to be "not with Him", making it clear that attributing Jesus' healing power to Satan was not only blasphemy against the Holy Spirit but the obvious *"bad fruit"* of a *"bad tree"*.

Bad trees are those that are not planted in (with) Jesus. Being with (planted in) Jesus is the only way we can see the difference between the works of the Holy Spirit and the degradation caused by demonic influence. It is the hardest thing for us to admit, but on our own we haven't got a clue. We will call wrong, right and right, wrong. Our track record proves we are blind and dumb, possessed by the evil spirit of a world in rebellion against its Creator. Thinking ourselves wise, we regularly choose darkness rather than light. Those verbal declarations of mistaken identity are going into an account and the owner of that account, Jesus says, will pay dearly.

He states clearly that if you are not with Him you are against Him; if you are not gathering with Him you are scattering. The context implies that it doesn't matter whether we think we know what we are saying or not. So much for sincerity covering a multitude of sins! We indeed can be sincerely WRONG!

MORE ON WHO IS JESUS?

With a patronizing tone and their pride bruised, the self-righteous politicians demand a sign. This may have been a knee-jerk attempt at wounding Jesus' credibility by putting Him on the spot to produce a sign at their command, but it just plays into His intention to disclose more about Himself. *"You evil and adulterous generation, you'll get your sign!"* He says it and attaches it to its historic real-life event which everyone in earshot knew from childhood: Jonah. *"The people he preached to repented, so they will sit in judgment on you because there is One here greater than Jonah! The Queen of the South came to hear the wisdom of Solomon, but a greater One than Solomon is right here, right now."* The principle that indicts them is the re-infestation that, by ever-increasing numbers and depravity of demons, invades those who act out the repentance-ritual over and over without actually surrendering their bodies to be the temple of the Holy Spirit - emptying but never being filled, tearing but never healing.

MORE ON WHO IS JESUS' FAMILY?

During Jesus' discourse, His mother Mary, and His (half) brothers came to the edge of the crowd and sent word that they wanted to speak to Him. Mark suggests in his journal that they were there to take Him home because they thought He had gone crazy (Mark 3:21). That only adds weight to His reply, which is the definitive answer to anyone who is unclear about the identity of Jesus' real Family. He had been modeling that same example all His life and for the third time that we know of, He sets His mom back on track.

I'm not familiar with how a Hebrew mom thinks, but it must have stung a little each time. The first was in the Temple where she found Him at 12 years old, *"How is it that you did not know where I would be and what I would be doing?"* The second was at the wedding party of a family friend where Mary presumed to push her Son out into the public eye, *"Woman, what are you doing? It's not my time yet."* This third time, she has allowed herself to be manipulated by her other sons to go save their family name. (Jesus had always been a stain on their reputation.)

Jesus doesn't even address her personally, but you can bet it stung when she watched Him stretch out His hand toward the disciples and heard from His own mouth, *"Behold! My mother and my brothers."* Then came the reminder of what she had lost sight of for a moment, *"For whoever is doing the desire of my Father, he is my brother; she is my sister, my mother."*

Chapter Fourteen

FOR DISCIPLES' EARS ONLY
Matthew 13:1-23

*L*ater that same day Jesus left the house and sat beside the lake. *A large crowd soon gathered around him, so he got into a boat. Then he sat there and taught as the people stood on the shore.*

He told many stories in the form of parables, such as this one: "Listen! A farmer went out to plant some seeds. As he scattered them across his field, some seeds fell on a footpath, and the birds came and ate them. Other seeds fell on shallow soil with underlying rock. The seeds sprouted quickly because the soil was shallow. But the plants soon wilted under the hot sun, and since they didn't have deep roots, they died. Other seeds fell among thorns that grew up and choked out the tender plants. Still other seeds fell on fertile soil, and they produced a crop that was thirty, sixty, and even a hundred times as much as had been planted! Anyone with ears to hear should listen and understand."

His disciples came and asked him, "Why do you use parables when you talk to the people?"

He replied, "You are permitted to understand the secrets of the Kingdom of Heaven, but others are not. To those who listen to my teaching, more understanding will be given, and they will have an abundance of knowledge. But for those who are not listening, even what little understanding they have will be taken away from them. That is why I use these parables,

For they look, but they don't really see.
They hear, but they don't really listen or understand.
This fulfills the prophecy of Isaiah that says,
'When you hear what I say,
you will not understand.
When you see what I do,
you will not comprehend.

For the hearts of these people are hardened,
and their ears cannot hear,
and they have closed their eyes—
so their eyes cannot see,
and their ears cannot hear,
and their hearts cannot understand,
and they cannot turn to me
and let me heal them.'

"But blessed are your eyes, because they see; and your ears, because they hear. I tell you the truth, many prophets and righteous people longed to see what you see, but they didn't see it. And they longed to hear what you hear, but they didn't hear it. "Now listen to the explanation of the parable about the farmer planting seeds: The seed that fell on the footpath represents those who hear the message about the Kingdom and don't understand it. Then the evil one comes and snatches away the seed that was planted in their hearts. The seed on the rocky soil represents those who hear the message and immediately receive it with joy. But since they don't have deep roots, they don't last long. They fall away as soon as they have problems or are persecuted for believing God's word. The seed that fell among the thorns represents those who hear God's word, but all too quickly the message is crowded out by the worries of this life and the lure of wealth, so no fruit is produced. The seed that fell on good soil represents those who truly hear and understand God's word and produce a harvest of thirty, sixty, or even a hundred times as much as had been planted!" (NLT)

The Seed Parable

This Farmer scatters Seed everywhere He goes and He goes everywhere! Where were you when Seed began to pelt your little head? Where were you when the Seed first penetrated the surface, and then when it began to take root? When did the Plant actually begin to grow? That patient Farmer just kept planting until it "took".

The Sower

Who is this Farmer? And how can He be so patient? It seems probable that the ultimate source of the Seed is God, supplying it by His Spirit to the distributors who scatter that Seed by their words and actions wherever God sends them. Of course, God has no need to hurry.

The Seed

The Word of God. The Gospel. The Good News. The message of the Kingdom. Confirmation that there is a loving Creator-God that rules in a Reality that is our real home and He has bought us out of slavery to the evil powers that presently hold this planet in darkness.

Wayside – Peripheral – Outside our reach

Our first exposure to this news of the Kingdom is just that - **new**. We are clueless. It practically goes in one ear and out the other. This also speaks of our state of mind, which is unable or unwilling to try to understand. We can't focus on it because it is so outside our mental rut.

Rocks - Compulsives & Hardheads

Stones in scripture mean established remembrances or dogma that block intelligent responsibility and growth. Conditions such as Rock-like, Hard-heartedness, Insensitivity, come to mind. This state of mind is typical of adolescence or in the early stages of character development. In that stage when we have just begun to learn, we tend to think we know everything. We are happy to hear the news, but we don't continue to focus on it because we don't want to. Our mind is made up and when the challenge comes, we retreat to business as usual.

Thorns - Worriers

The descriptive words used here draw a picture of people who by their own choice are beat up, kidnapped and suffocated. Like the thorns of a thick bush, these poor souls are pointed in every direction. They cannot focus on anything because they are so fractured, there is no way to tell which way is up.

Good Ground - Broken, Prepared & Hungry

The good ground here is beautiful and well prepared for its purpose. This condition of the heart is in stark contrast to the other ground upon which the Seed fell. In the description of this ground's receiving of the Seed there is an element of drawing the Seed into itself. This suggests an active seeking after the Seed.

Why Parables?

When these different types of ground are perceived as stages of the Word penetrating into our hearts we can also see the confirmation and illustration of the concept that it is God who is the *pursuer* as in John 4:23 and that it is His Spirit that "*works in us to will and to do...*"(Phil 2:13). When seen in this light the reason Jesus gives for telling things in parables makes sense (see Isaiah 6:9-10).

Disciples' Access

"But blessed [are] your eyes, for they see; and your ears, for they hear." This blessing was due in large part to the fact that Jesus is going to explain the parables to them personally. There seems to be more than just the obvious advantage of having a person tell us face to face what they meant by what they have said. Jesus suggests this in verses 11-12, *"Because it is given unto you to know the mysteries of the kingdom of heaven, but to them it is not given. For whosoever hath, to him shall be given, and he shall have more abundance; but whosoever hath not, from him shall be taken away even that he hath."* So having this privileged access to the substance of the reign of God's Kingdom guarantees that we will never see the stream of information and insight dry up.

How Do I Qualify?

(John 14:6-7) *Jesus said to him, I am the way, the truth, and the life; no man comes to the Father, but by me. If you had known me, you should have known my Father also; and from now on you know him, and have seen him* (v15). *If you love me, keep my commandments* (v21-27). *He that has my commandments, and keeps them, he it is that loves me; and he that loves me shall be loved of my Father, and I will love him, and will manifest myself to him. Judas said to him, not Iscariot, "Lord, how is it that you will manifest yourself to us, and not to the world?" Jesus answered and said to him, If a man love me, he will keep my words; and my Father will love him, and we will come to him, and make our abode with him. He that does not love me does not keep my sayings; and the word which you hear is not mine, but the Father's which sent me. These things have I spoken to you, being [yet] present with you. But the Comforter, [which is] the Holy Ghost, whom the Father will send in my name, he shall teach you all things, and bring all things to your remembrance, whatsoever I have said to you. Peace I leave with you, my peace I give to you; not as the world gives, give I to you. Let not your heart be troubled, neither let it be afraid.*

We qualify if we love Jesus, which is verified by the fact that we do what He says. [That is the reason for this journal; so we will get familiar with what He says and do it the way He wants to do it – in our skin.]

NOTE: That last statement Jesus makes in John 14:27 should not be read in a sappy, sympathetic voice: "No men, I hope you won't feel upset or afraid [sniffle]." No – this is a *command*: "Since you have this privileged, constant access to Me, My Father and our perspective and insight, stop letting yourselves be manipulated and pushed around by circumstances and the influence of this world. Live and walk with Me, in My peace, My love, power and sanity."

Chapter Fifteen

THE MIXED CROP PLOY
Matthew 13:24-30

[NOTE: the parenthesis (...) shows Jesus' own interpretation
from the later verses]

*A*nother parable he set before them, saying, "The kingdom
of heaven is like a man (Jesus, v37) who sowed good seed
(children of the kingdom, v38) in his field (the world, v38):
But while men slept, his enemy (the devil, v39) *came and sowed tares*
(children of the wicked one, v38) *among the wheat, and went his way."*
[This was likely darnel or rye grass which grows in grain fields. The
name was formerly given to any weed growing in grain.]

"But when the grain had sprouted, and produced a crop, then the
tares also appeared.

*"So the servants of the owner came and said to him, Sir, did you
not sow good seed in your field? How then does it have tares?*

*"He said to them, An enemy has done this. The servants said to
him, Do you want us then to go and gather them up?*

*"But he said, No, lest while you gather up the tares you also uproot
up the wheat with them.*

"Let both grow together until the harvest (end of the age, v39),
and at the time of harvest I will say to the reapers (the angels, v39),
*First gather together the tares and bind them in bundles to burn them,
but gather the wheat into my barn."* (NKJV)

Have you ever wondered at the way evil seems to go unpunished
even among Christians? Impostors flourish and it seems that God
doesn't notice. In verse 28 and 29 the servants came to Him and asked
the question, "How did this happen?" Then they offer to go take care of
the problem. We are always ready to take care of those little impostors
for God, aren't we? Note how He replies, "No, you'll just kill off some of

the good guys along with them. Just leave them alone and I'll take care of it at harvest time."

Jesus is the One who has been given all authority in the judgment department. The thing that makes Him take care of things a little differently than we expect is that He has this directive from the Father: I don't want any of My children to perish. If He rooted up the impostors before we are ripe for Harvest, some of us would be rooted up, too.

We might be thinking, "I'm already being uprooted by these con artists, these wolves in sheep's clothing!"

There are only two things to say to that:

1) We can't afford thinking we know enough to do the judging for Jesus. We can't take the time out of what we are supposed to be doing to judge someone based on the limited insight we have.

2) We can't afford to confuse our present trials, no matter how devastating, with being uprooted. Remember the apostles and all the others who endured persecution, torture and death.

They didn't just have a hard time getting along. They didn't just get depressed or have a nervous breakdown. They weren't just slandered or humiliated. They were tortured to death. Did that uproot them? No! They endured all that for the deep soul-joy of being eternally rooted in Yeshua their Messiah.

So then, what is the point? If the outcome (or crop) is going to be the same either way, what is the purpose of the "tares"? Let's look at it from the devil's point of view for a moment. What would he be trying to prove? He must know better than to think that mixing weeds in with God's wheat is going to actually turn any of the wheat stalks into weeds. No, from the devil's perspective, this is at best a malicious prank just to cause confusion, choke off some of the growth and add more to the work of growing and harvesting the wheat.

Now, let's look from God's view. That's always where the real fun begins! Oh, but before we do, let me ask this question: Has the devil ever surprised God? From what we know of God and His Book, it's obvious that the devil is a very predictable egomaniac whose antics always end up playing into God's ultimate plan for His children.

If God knew that the devil would be sneaking in and pulling that prank, why didn't He stop him? He could have saved Himself a lot of work. The discussion of this could fill volumes but let me just open one corner of God's goodie-bag and see what comes out.

The very thing that would actually cause the confusion in the beginning is what makes everything clear in the end. The devil didn't plant dandelions in the wheat. The field workers would have noticed that the minute the first leaf was formed. No, the plant of choice was one that looked just like wheat right up to when the fruit was supposed to appear. At that point its roots were fully grown and it took up just as much space as the wheat stalk, but no fruit was formed in the flower. Instead, the flower would turn a telltale color and just hang out - continuing to "act" like wheat but now everyone knows the truth. At least, everyone with eyes and ears open (see Matthew 7:15-27).

YOU BECOME THE SEED OF WHAT IS PLANTED IN YOU

Let's not dwell on the devil's objectives. They're not worth the time it takes to mention them. Jesus said the seeds are people. By the way, seeds grow up to be plants after they have died and are buried. These people/seeds form two very distinct groups. But God allows the bad and the good seed to grow in the same earth side-by-side. I'm sure I could never know all the reasons why, but the list needs to start with practicalities like, how else would we know the difference? I mean how, other than by contrast, could God show us some of the subtle differences between wrong and right, evil and righteousness? But wait! His purpose is not to teach us how to discerningly focus on other people's faults. His goal is to show us Himself, so that we will come to know Him. I am confident that every point we would rightly make concerning God's purposes for us would come down to that - that we might know Him - since that's the definition of the "eternal" [perpetually refreshed] life He wants to give us (see John 17:3).

Chapter Sixteen

ROOTED & TREASURED IN HIM
Matthew 13:31-35 & 44-52

*H*ere is another illustration Jesus used: "The Kingdom of Heaven is like a mustard seed planted in a field. It is the smallest of all seeds, but it becomes the largest of garden plants; it grows into a tree, and birds come and make nests in its branches."

Jesus also used this illustration: "The Kingdom of Heaven is like the yeast a woman used in making bread. Even though she put only a little yeast in three measures of flour, it permeated every part of the dough." (NLT)

Jesus always used stories and illustrations like these when speaking to the crowds. In fact, he never spoke to them without using such parables. This fulfilled what God had spoken through the prophet:

"I will speak to you in parables. I will explain things hidden since the creation of the world."

"The Kingdom of Heaven is like a treasure that a man discovered hidden in a field. In his excitement, he hid it again and sold everything he owned to get enough money to buy the field.

"Again, the Kingdom of Heaven is like a merchant on the lookout for choice pearls. When he discovered a pearl of great value, he sold everything he owned and bought it!

"Again, the Kingdom of Heaven is like a fishing net that was thrown into the water and caught fish of every kind. When the net was full, they dragged it up onto the shore, sat down, and sorted the good fish into crates, but threw the bad ones away. That is the way it will be at the end of the world. The angels will come and separate the wicked people from the righteous, throwing the wicked into the fiery furnace, where there will be weeping and gnashing of teeth. Do you understand all these things?"

"Yes," they said, "we do."

Then he added, "Every teacher of religious law who becomes a disciple in the Kingdom of Heaven is like a homeowner who brings from his storeroom new gems of truth as well as old."

verse 31 - 32 • A man took a mustard seed and planted it. The Kingdom is like the seed. It is small and grows to a significant, even disproportionate size compared to other seed/plant ratios.
    Action: taken and planted.
    Motive: to grow, produce herbs and lodging.

verse 33 • A woman took leaven and hid it in meal. The Kingdom is like the leaven. The leaven spread through the 3 measures of meal.
    Action: taken and hidden.
    Motive: to spread and permeate.

verse 44 • A man discovered a treasure chest in a field. He hid it, sold all he had and bought the field. The Kingdom is like the treasure. It is only his if he owns the whole piece of land. It is assumed that what he pays for the field is a fraction of the value of the treasure.
    Action: discovered, hid and bought.
    Motive: to own and be provided for

verse 45 - 46 • A merchant found the pearl of his dreams, sold all he owned and bought it. The Kingdom is like the merchant.
    Action: discover, sell out and buy.
    Motive: to own and behold.

verse 47 - 50 • A net was cast in the sea that gathered everything. The Kingdom is the net. Then they (angels v48) pulled it ashore and separated the clean from the unclean. Jesus says this is a picture of the end of the age.
    Action: cast in, gather and separate.
    Motive: completion of the age, gather all who are fit to enter God's full Reality.

Verse 35 says Jesus is revealing through these parables secrets that have been untold from the foundation of the earth (see Ps 78:2).

Verse 52 implies that understanding these parables is like becoming the head of a family, bound by duty to embrace or guard even by force, holding final authority to judge everything, old or new.

This is a pretty heavy proposition! Many of us have a natural tendency to assume that kind of authority without hesitation, ignoring the fact that our judgment doesn't actually change anything. Authority is something we all want, but authority is bestowed – commissioned. It is not self-assumed. Even Jesus, the Son of God Himself, says, "*I have been GIVEN authority...*" (Matt 28:18+). To think that a bestowed authority from God would actually be connected with understanding these parables makes me search very hard for keys that would unlock their deep fountains of truth.

In that search I have seen several connective strings of relationship in these word pictures that have continued to draw me deeper into the search. One of those strings is the "hidden" nature of the initial part of each one. There's the seed that is hidden by planting, the leaven that is hidden in meal, the treasure hidden in the field. These three are described as hidden with the idea that they will become visible. In growing a crop, the planting always comes before reaping. The initial stage involves hard work with nothing much to show for it except freshly broken soil. The seed becomes a tree, the leaven spreads, and the treasure is found and secured. The merchant is willing, as is the dragnet, to obtain everything rather than risk losing or damaging the treasure.

REFLECTIONS TO SHARE?

Maybe you have some thoughts on these parables that you would like to share. How is the Kingdom of Heaven like a mustard seed or leaven or discovered treasure? How does it work like a merchant or a net? I would enjoy reading your insights. Connect at CatalystPeople. com.

Chapter Seventeen

OLD MAN vs. NEW MAN
Matthew 13:53-14:36

We will now read Matthew 13:53ff - 14:36, and take the first point from the last 6 verses of chapter 13. Then we will take the second point from the words Jesus speaks to His freaked-out disciples in 14:27. At that point we will step back and get the whole passage in view.

13:53ff (CJB) *When Jesus had finished telling these stories and illustrations, he left that part of the country. He returned to Nazareth, his hometown. When he taught there in the synagogue, everyone was amazed and said, "Where does he get this wisdom and the power to do miracles?" Then they scoffed, "He's just the carpenter's son, and we know Miryam, his mother, and his brothers—Ya'akov, Yosef, Shim'on and Y'hudah? All his sisters live right here among us. Where did he learn all these things?" And they were deeply offended and refused to believe in him. Then Jesus told them, "A prophet is honored everywhere except in his own hometown and among his own family." And so he did only a few miracles there because of their unbelief.*

This has always been a bit painful for me to read. People from Jesus' own hometown (Nazareth) were <u>offended</u>? But, for a long time I hadn't even asked aloud why they responded like that. I guess Jesus' own words were strong enough to relieve me from any personal soul searching. To me it sounded like, "That's just the way it is for a prophet." Actually though, I think it might be healthy to ask out loud...

If "that's just the way it is", is the explanation, why did those people – why would anyone – take offense at a hometown boy coming back with that kind of authority and power? Fear? Pride? Jealousy? How do I feel when a childhood friend of mine makes an accomplishment or gets an advancement of some kind, that I would never even be able to aspire to? Do I naturally feel happy for them or is there a tiny impish voice whispering in the back of my mind, "He's just not one of us any more," or, "She must think she's really hot stuff now!"

An old saying about personally convicting discoveries says, "If the shoe fits, wear it." But Paul doesn't tell us to do that. He says, when we notice that imp poke its head up, "Put off the old man and put on the new man, even Christ Jesus" (see Romans 5:17-6:18, Ephesians 4:21-5:5, Colossians 3:9-10). Let the Holy Spirit's surgical Light shine deep into our hearts. Let Him do the work that self-discipline can't do, especially when we would rather say, "That's just the way it is."

14:1-36 (NLT) *When Herod Antipas, the ruler of Galilee, heard about Jesus, he said to his advisers, "This must be John the Baptist raised from the dead! That is why he can do such miracles." For Herod had arrested and imprisoned John as a favor to his wife Herodias (the former wife of Herod's brother, Philip). John had been telling Herod, "It is against God's law for you to marry her." Herod wanted to kill John, but he was afraid of a riot, because all the people believed John was a prophet.*

But at a birthday party for Herod, Herodias's daughter performed a dance that greatly pleased him, so he promised with a vow to give her anything she wanted. At her mother's urging, the girl said, "I want the head of John the Baptist on a tray!" Then the king regretted what he had said; but because of the vow he had made in front of his guests, he issued the necessary orders. So John was beheaded in the prison, and his head was brought on a tray and given to the girl, who took it to her mother. Later, John's disciples came for his body and buried it. Then they went and told Jesus what had happened.

As soon as Jesus heard the news, he left in a boat to a remote area to be alone. But the crowds heard where he was headed and followed on foot from many towns. Jesus saw the huge crowd as he stepped from the boat, and he had compassion on them and healed their sick.

That evening the disciples came to him and said, "This is a remote place, and it's already getting late. Send the crowds away so they can go to the villages and buy food for themselves."

Jesus said, "That isn't necessary — you feed them."

"But we have only five loaves of bread and two fish!" they answered.

"Bring them here," he said. Then he told the people to sit down on the grass. Jesus took the five loaves and two fish, looked up toward heaven, and blessed them. Then, breaking the loaves into pieces, he gave the bread to the disciples, who distributed it to the people. They all ate as much as they wanted, and afterward, the disciples picked up twelve baskets of leftovers. About 5,000 men were fed that day, in addition to all the women and children!

Immediately after this, Jesus insisted that his disciples get back into the boat and cross to the other side of the lake, while he sent the people home. After sending them home, he went up into the hills by himself to pray. Night fell while he was there alone

Meanwhile, the disciples were in trouble far away from land, for a strong wind had risen, and they were fighting heavy waves. About three o'clock in the morning Jesus came toward them, walking on the water. When the disciples saw him walking on the water, they were terrified. In their fear, they cried out, "It's a ghost!"

But Jesus spoke to them at once. "Don't be afraid," he said. "Take courage. I am here!" Then Peter called to him, "Lord, if it's really you, tell me to come to you, walking on the water." "Yes, come," Jesus said.

So Peter went over the side of the boat and walked on the water toward Jesus. But when he saw the strong wind and the waves, he was terrified and began to sink. "Save me, Lord!" he shouted. Jesus immediately reached out and grabbed him. "You have so little faith," Jesus said. "Why did you doubt me?"

When they climbed back into the boat, the wind stopped. Then the disciples worshiped him. "You really are the Son of God!" they exclaimed.

After they had crossed the lake, they landed at Gennesaret. When the people recognized Jesus, the news of his arrival spread quickly throughout the whole area, and soon people were bringing all their sick to be healed. They begged him to let the sick touch at least the fringe of his robe, and all who touched him were healed.

In this passage we are reminded that in the real world there's: Bad people, Bad government, Bad conscience, Bad decisions, Bad promises, Bad breaks, Bad news, Bad planning, Bad places, Bad timing, Bad feelings, Bad storms.

"There's: Unbelief, Deceit, Persecution, Conspiracy, Murder, Grief, Fear, Disease.

BUT JESUS SAYS, "Oh, cheer up boys. It's Me! Don't be so fearful."

Doesn't that sound a bit like Proverbs 3:6 - *In all thy ways acknowledge (know, learn to know, perceive and see, find out and discern, discriminate, distinguish) him, and he shall direct (right, straighten, level) thy paths (way of living)* [AMP].

I wonder how many Christians today continue to be confused about how they should look at the things that are happening to them? Constantly I hear stories of what has been done by "the enemy," the devil, Satan, demons and "the god of this world." They are given credit for circumstances and events that are seen as negative or depressing, or even just a little different from the way we expect them to be. Acknowledgment of God at work seems to occur almost exclusively when the event is immediately seen as positive, pleasing or fortunate in some way.

That makes me uncomfortable, especially in light of the panorama of Scripture and the history of God's interaction with His people. We seem to have somehow gotten the idea, like them, that being "blessed by God" means that the powers of heaven supernaturally shroud us and protect us from all "negative" forces and events. If we hold that view and the shroud is spoiled by something negative, and it will be, we will live in fear and denial.

"I have told you all this so that you may have peace in me. Here on earth you will have many trials and sorrows. But take heart, because I have overcome the world. (John 16:33 NLT)"

Doesn't it sound a little too much like voodoo? Doesn't it seem adolescent, even arrogant to call out demonic forces in order to engage in some kind of verbal pugilism or ritual power play? Can it really matter what the world or even the devil himself does to me if my complete trust and confidence is in my Father, the Creator-God? Well, can it? The real demonstration of the power of God in us is in how we live our daily lives in the midst of even the worst turmoil that evil can throw at us. Acting like we have personal authority over the forces of evil is not what will make it so, no matter how many people we convince. Jesus is the One with all authority and only as we absolutely lean on and rest in Jesus and the unlimited power of His Spirit, will we enjoy actually experiencing such phenomena. It will obviously be His hand we see moving; His power displayed.

If we have been drawn into this preoccupation with "discerning" and "warring" against the activities of Satan, then the Holy Spirit's challenge to us is to allow Jesus to show us what is happening beyond that superficial level of Satan's fictitious facade. Of course, everything the devil does is dirty and nasty. Of course, Jesus has the power to overcome the dirtiest and nastiest that the devil can come up with. BUT – the good news is that He already HAS overcome the devil and ALL his works. The question now is, will we place our unreserved trust in that? If that is our desire then we will exert a little more effort to apply that truth to the postures we take in conversation, relationship, prayer, worship and the daily activities of our lives.

The last words of this passage are "As many as touched (His

garment) were made PERFECTLY WHOLE." What exactly does that mean? Jesus is clearly able to change the bad stuff of life but He didn't come to clean up the world and straighten it out. He came to "seek and to save that which was lost" (Luke 19:10). Many of us would be shocked to know what Jesus' actual point of view and objectives are. God's ultimate goal is not to make our lives more comfortable or rescue us from the ugly plots of the devil.

Some of us may question this piece of news, but it is clear that His agenda goes far beyond that. In fact some of us have built our presuppositions of God on such a humanistic, self-centered philosophy that we cannot even read the Old Testament. We haven't got the stomach for it. Maybe you have thought, "There is just too much suffering and too many times I can't justify God's actions." That is a strong hint that we simply do not know God or have a clue what He is up to. The Bible is very clear about what humans are up to. We are seeking our own comfort and personal power over the environment and people. Jesus said that God is seeking genuine worshipers... Jesus came seeking the "lost."

Would we say we are "the lost?" Many of us will recoil in self-defense because we culturally connect that with being "bad people." But changing bad people or bad breaks and the sort, didn't seem to be Jesus' goal as we read Matthew 14. Was His time and energy consumed with our brand of righteousness which, for example, would have found a way to bring Herod to justice, among others? Clearly no.

We see Him grieving for His cousin and regenerating alone with His Father. We see Him healing and feeding and rescuing lost, confused, hurting and frightened people - the victims of all those bad things in the real world. Sometimes He changed physical circumstances but most of the time He was, and still is, dealing with people - personally. They were His from the beginning. They were lost. He came that we, His lost children, could be rescued from this world's rebellion and reconciled back to our Father; to be reinstated members of His Family...then to be in this world as fiber optics.

As with fiber optics the source-light may be geographically far away but the intensity is as if it is "close at hand." Jesus wants to be personally shining on those at whom we smile, mending the brokenhearted, encouraging the hopeless. But we must choose. Which will be our vocation? Fixing the bad things, waging war on the nasty (already defeated) enemy, campaigning for justice? Or will we be about what Jesus is about? If we really want to overcome evil, let's do it the Biblical way - Romans 12:21, *"Be not overcome by evil, but overcome evil with good.*" Direct-and-personal. One-on-one. Just like Jesus. God initiates good and evil tries but cannot overcome it.

POSTSCRIPT

As I write these words, prayerfully disclosing the heart of Jesus and the intentions of God, many nations and people are being consumed by a wave of evil and corruption that is exposing the beginning of the end for Satan's delusion of dominion. What I have written must not be taken as license for not speaking out and taking action to stand openly for the freedom in Jesus for which God has designed us, and for which Jesus has bought us out of Satan's slave market. No matter how bleak the circumstances or the cost of standing for righteousness, it is our duty and responsibility as citizens of God's Kingdom, who have been sent and given to be the light of this world, to hold the Word of God above all that would exalt itself above it.

Chapter Eighteen

CULTURAL RULES vs. GOD'S RULES
Matthew 15:1-20

*T*hen *the scribes and Pharisees who were from Jerusalem came to Jesus, saying, "Why do Your disciples transgress the tradition of the elders? For they do not wash their hands when they eat bread."*

He answered and said to them, "Why do you also transgress the commandment of God because of your tradition?

"For God commanded, saying, 'Honor your father and your mother'; and, 'He who curses father or mother, let him be put to death.' But you say, 'Whoever says to his father or mother, whatever profit you might have received from me is a gift to God -- then he need not honor his father or mother.' Thus you have made the commandment of God of no effect by your tradition.

"Hypocrites! Well did Isaiah prophesy about you, saying: 'These people draw near to Me with their mouth, And honor Me with their lips, But their heart is far from Me. And in vain they worship Me, Teaching as doctrines the commandments of men.'"

When He had called the multitude to Himself, He said to them, "Hear and understand: Not what goes into the mouth defiles a man; but what comes out of the mouth, this defiles a man."

Then His disciples came and said to Him, "Do You know that the Pharisees were offended when they heard this saying?" But He answered and said, "Every plant which My heavenly Father has not planted will be uprooted. Let them alone. They are blind leaders of the blind. And if the blind leads the blind, both will fall into a ditch."

Then Peter answered and said to Him, "Explain this parable to us."

So Jesus said, "Are you also still without understanding? Do you not yet understand that whatever enters the mouth goes into the stomach and is eliminated? But those things which proceed out of the mouth come from the heart, and they defile a man. For out of the heart proceed evil thoughts, murders, adulteries, fornications, thefts, false witness, and blasphemies. These are the things which defile a man, but to eat with unwashed hands does not defile a man." (NKJV)

Sometimes when reading or hearing Jesus talking to the twelve, I catch myself thinking, "That's a little rude!" Reading again Matt 15:15-16, Peter, after hearing His teaching (v10-14) asks Him to explain. Jesus replies, in essence, "Are you still spiritually deaf?" It suddenly occurred to me, that before He had ascended and He and the Father sent the Other, The Explainer, Teacher, He uses a very different method of teaching with His inner circle of disciples, which includes a tool called "antagonism." You could say, Jesus was using "pre-antagonism," because He knows all too well there will be plenty antagonism to come. Then, He graciously continues to upload the explanation or carries out the needed intervention. So, it is clearly a tool being used, not a demeaning criticism. But this inserted training method exposes our need to put the mind He's given us to use, in sync with the Spirit's insight to *"hear AND understand" His* message behind everything we encounter through our senses in a routine day (see Matt 13:13), and accept the challenge.

We desperately need to catch the depth of how Jesus felt about the religious leaders teaching man's rules as if they were God's laws. This is one of several times when the hyper-religious and self-righteous provide their stark contrast to the pure righteousness and power of Jesus. Those events are in scripture so we can learn how to deal with that disease in ourselves as well as in others. A super-practical point of view is called for when dealing with super-spiritual motives and actions, and there has lived on earth no human more practical than Jesus. When superficial things attain sacred status, there is clearly a super-identity problem.

IDENTIFICATION PLEASE
When God gave Moses the instructions for worship and the layout for the Tabernacle it was to start clearing up Israel's identity problem. But it was only the beginning of the process. Continuing to give our allegiance to objects and rituals after discovering the person of Jesus, the One to whom all those objects and rituals were designed to lead us, clearly signals either a severe mental problem or just willful ignorance.

The last thing I want to hear Jesus say to me is, "Hey, Stupid!" Does that sentence cause discomfort? If we think Jesus doesn't talk like that, we will need to edit the Book we're reading. And believe me, that is a common practice historically. The appropriate reaction is that it makes us want to take inventory of things we think are "sacred" and make absolutely sure that He agrees.

We must ask ourselves:

1.) How much of my identity or my identification of others comes from my impressions of superficial actions or looks – mode of dress, hairstyle, race, accent, etc.? Does the tone of someone's voice or elevated language, or the fact they are on TV, identify them as a godly person? Am *I* identified by the clothes *I* wear or the car I drive or the house *I* live in? Do I identify certain styles of music as "Christian" or "non-Christian?" Is there a "dress code," beyond the boundaries of modesty, that makes it clear I am "in church?"

2.) How much of my identity or my identification of others comes from Jesus' identification? Not my cultural interpretation of Jesus, but the real, living Jesus. KNOWING HIM is our identification with "eternal life."

That "KNOWING" is exactly what we're looking at here – identifying with Jesus in every aspect of life and personality. It seems safe to say that at some point each of us has confidently done something that we thought would be what someone would want us to do, only to find that we were wrong. The smart response to that situation would be to learn from it to get more familiar with people, so we could avoid making that mistake again. It's silly to continue to guess and fake it. Well, isn't it? Especially when intimate relationship with Him is our very Life. AND it is freely available and so near, even within us!

Intimacy is what Jesus was born, lived a human life, died, rose again and lives right now to make available to us. That eternal lifestyle has nothing to do with just guessing and faking it or mindlessly following churchy cultural rules, which, in every society in history, has eventually buried the reality and vibrant life of the Church. Look it up. There's a Book, look everything up. Verify all.

Let's seal this session with recalling Jesus' direct response to that guess-and-fake-it kind of religious person in verses 13-14: "Every tree that wasn't planted by my Father in heaven will be pulled up by its roots. Forget them. They are blind men leading blind men. When a blind man leads a blind man, they both end up in the ditch."

Want to stay out of the ditch? Get better acquainted with the Truth, the Way, the Life, the Prince of Peace, the Mighty God, the

Everlasting Father, the Savior and Light of the world, the Friend who is closer than a brother, who gave and was given so that we could be His child and He could be our God and Father; that we could KNOW HIM and worship Him in the beauty of holiness! [*set apart* for Him and His agenda in those with whom He has planted us.]

Chapter Nineteen

MAN WITH A MISSION
Matthew 15:21-28

*T*hen *Jesus left Galilee and went north to the region of Tyre and Sidon. A Gentile woman who lived there came to him, pleading, "Have mercy on me, O Lord, Son of David! For my daughter is possessed by a demon that torments her severely."*

But Jesus gave her no reply, not even a word. Then his disciples urged him to send her away. "Tell her to go away," they said. "She is bothering us with all her begging."

Then Jesus said to the woman, "I was sent only to help God's lost sheep—the people of Israel."

But she came and worshiped him, pleading again, "Lord, help me!"

Jesus responded, "It isn't right to take food from the children and throw it to the dogs."

She replied, "That's true, Lord, but even dogs are allowed to eat the scraps that fall beneath their master's table."

"Dear woman," Jesus said to her, "your faith is great. Your request is granted." And her daughter was instantly healed. (NLT)

On the Mediterranean coast a "Canaanite" woman persistently follows Jesus' itinerant team and hounds them with her cries for help for her daughter who is horribly tormented by a demon. Jesus ignores her.

Our natural reaction may be, "What? That's not the Jesus I know!" That's because the naked truth is that there are so many ways we do *not* know Him. *"My thoughts are not your thoughts, nor are your ways my ways... For as the heavens are higher than the earth, so are my ways higher than your ways and my thoughts higher than your thoughts"* (Isaiah 55:8-9).

This is one of those crossroads that Jesus brings us to that we must engage and move with Him or we will not go on. It calls to mind the surprising introduction of words like "eat my flesh and drink my Blood"(John 6:53-56). There was pretty significant fall-out from that. John 6:66: *"From that time many of His disciples went back and walked with Him no more."* The point is that many turned away in disgust, maybe like ours when we heard His response to the Canaanite woman's cry for help. After all, these Jews had strict rules about eating certain things and drinking blood, but they really did *not* know Jesus. Once we are immersed in Him, *knowing* eclipses all our cluelessness. He said Himself, "I didn't come to bring peace but a sword" (Matt 10:34), and that's His own clue to His motivation.

My question is this: Does Jesus have ulterior motives or secret agendas? Technically speaking, I guess we could say yes, just because we haven't got a clue what He's doing most of the time. But, would He even think to give reasons for His words and actions that relate to our human reasoning in order to get our loyalty? Once we are sure the translation of His words is correct, we must take what Jesus says and does at face value. Our responsibility is to hear Him, ask His Spirit in us for understanding, and then by His empowerment, defer to Him, without trying to align Him to our uninformed picture of Him.

Did He really ignore this woman? Yes. Why? He Himself articulated the reason very clearly, *"I was sent..."* The disciples didn't ask Him why He was ignoring her. They were irritated by her wailing and begged Him to get rid of her. "Jesus, please tell her to go away, she's bothering us!"

To their request, still not to her, Jesus says, *"I am sent... to the lost sheep of Israel and to no one else."* His mission was very specific and He was exclusively driven by that mission, not by the temporal needs of people. Yes, like it or not. Though He would feel those needs like no one else could, He was going to say what He heard the Father say and do what He saw the Father do, even though it was going to kill Him. He was focused and driven by His complete abandon to the Father's desire and commission, which meant torture and death before the finish line.

Jesus' lack of response to this woman's cry for help had nothing to do with a disregard for her need or prejudice toward her race or blood line. He was not calling her a "dog" when He said, *"It is not right to throw a child's bread to dogs."* Here's a more accurate interpretation, backed up by her comeback to what He says to her, "You don't give a puppy the food your child needs!" There was and is a very specific "diet" by which to raise the house of Israel [to redemption], as there is a specific and different one for raising the gentiles, as well as a different time frame by the way.

She has a great comeback, "Absolutely, Master! But puppies get the crumbs that fall from their master's table." Meaning, "All that would be necessary to heal my daughter is a tiny morsel of your great power to heal and save her and my breaking heart. You wouldn't even notice it was gone." Probably with a glimmer of a smile, He said something like, "Wow woman, you've got some big faith. You have what you ask!" Her daughter was healed from that moment.

Chapter Twenty

MAN WITH COMPASSION
Matthew 15:29-39

*A*nd Jesus departed from there, skirted the Sea of Galilee, and went up on the mountain and sat down there. Then great mul-titudes came to Him, having with them those who were lame, blind, mute, maimed, and many others; and they laid them down at Jesus' feet, and He healed them. So the multitude marveled when they saw the mute speaking, the maimed made whole, the lame walking, and the blind seeing; and they glorified the God of Israel.

Then Jesus called His disciples to Him and said, "I have compassion on the multitude, because they have now continued with Me three days and have nothing to eat. And I do not want to send them away hungry, lest they faint on the way."

Then His disciples said to Him, "Where could we get enough bread in the wilderness to fill such a great multitude?"

Jesus said to them, "How many loaves do you have?"

And they said, "Seven, and a few little fish."

And He commanded the multitude to sit down on the ground. And He took the seven loaves and the fish and gave thanks, broke them and gave them to His disciples; and the disciples gave to the multitude. So they all ate and were filled, and they took up seven large baskets full of the fragments that were left. Now those who ate were four thousand men, besides women and children. And He sent away the multitude, got into the boat, and came to the region of Magdala.(NKJV)

Only the person who has the resources and the intent to meet a need can afford to have compassion. Without those a person can only afford sympathy, which, frankly, is hardly worth the effort - for either side. Jesus is fully aware of His resources and without posturing or fanfare, puts those resources to work in our lives

Once His heart is installed in us and we are fully committed to defer to Him, the resources of Heaven are at our disposal. Notice the pivotal phrase, *His heart.* That is where we need to look. That's what we need to focus on.

In Biblical context, a Christian is a person who is totally possessed by the nature of their Creator-Father, made possible by Jesus, carried out by His invisible, indwelling, personal self – His Spirit. That doesn't change even if it is a derogatory slam, as with the disgusted Roman soldiers who coined the nickname. It is still the same definition. Are you a clone of Jesus? Guilty as charged!

Therefore, Jesus' point of view is what the Christian chooses to dictate his or her thoughts and actions. He can now begin to manifest His life in our human flesh because that's the life we're living, as out loud as possible. Our primary determination is to know and defer to Him, as He shows Himself in the face of every situation we meet.

The problem is that unless that is happening, we will misunderstand EVERYTHING. Yes, everything. We may not even know what the challenge of a situation really is. The sooner we force ourselves to install the habit of turning to Jesus and asking for His perspective, the sooner we can begin to enjoy the life He wants to live in us.

I'll venture a personal illustration. When I was released from the psych ward in Munich, Germany, I walked out of the hospital with a brand new, un-programed brain. Jesus' voice and revelation of His reason for becoming a human being had given me a rational reason for being one. But almost everything had to be learned. The physical instincts to walk and eat, etc., were present. But relational interactions and words, their meanings and how they work in relation to one another in daily life, even the continuity of a sentence, had to be given definition and purpose. So, every time I encountered the need for personal engagement in actions or words, I would immediately look at Jesus with the standard question, "What? What does that mean and am I supposed to respond?" I wore an imprint of my little backside into the step beside His feet because there is no other place to go for rational reasoning, so that was and is forever my home. I wrote in the first of these pages that from the day of my choice to go back into the world of humans with Jesus, He was and always will be my only sanity. I saw the world's own "sanity" being carried to its logical conclusion, ending in totalitarian chaos, anarchy and the judgment of Almighty God. That is *insanity* seen through our Creator and Savior's eyes. And He sees it all. But...

He doesn't, on heroic impulse, jump into a disastrous situation and fake it. Nor does He throw up His hands in sympathy and give up. Those both come out of the nature of cut off, confused and broken humans. He has us in this world and these situations, in this family and these awkward positions, to give us a view of Him we have not ever seen before. He wants us to defer to Him, then watch and enjoy how He uses His resources through our surrendered bodies. "...*learn of me...*" "*My yoke is easy...*" (Matt 11:28-30 ESV). The yoke we are in with Him is the one that He, the master carpenter, designed and made specifically to fit us and Him, to do all that He has designed us to do – together. I'll name only a few – learning, growing, working, plowing, planting, harvesting, failing, falling, getting up, running, preaching (sometimes even with words), mentoring, living every minute and every experience – TOGETHER.

And remember, whatever resource He has put in our hand, that's enough. Don't grip it. Give it, serving with Him. He will bless it, break it and do abundantly above what we ask or even imagine.

Chapter Twenty One

SHOW US A SIGN!
Matthew 16:1-20

*O*ne day the Pharisees and Sadducees came to test Jesus, de-
manding that he show them a miraculous sign from heaven
to prove his authority. He replied, "You know the saying, 'Red
sky at night means fair weather tomorrow; red sky in the morning
means foul weather all day.' You know how to interpret the weather
signs in the sky, but you don't know how to interpret the signs of the
times! Only an evil, adulterous generation would demand a miraculous sign, but the only sign I will give them is the sign of the prophet
Jonah." Then Jesus left them and went away.*

*Later, after they crossed to the other side of the lake, the disciples
discovered they had forgotten to bring any bread. "Watch out!" Jesus
warned them. "Beware of the yeast of the Pharisees and Sadducees."*

*At this they began to argue with each other because they hadn't
brought any bread. Jesus knew what they were saying, so he said,
"You have so little faith! Why are you arguing with each other
about having no bread? Don't you understand even yet? Don't you
remember the 5,000 I fed with five loaves, and the baskets of leftovers
you picked up? Or the 4,000 I fed with seven loaves, and the large
baskets of leftovers you picked up? Why can't you understand that I'm
not talking about bread? So again I say, 'Beware of the yeast of the
Pharisees and Sadducees.'" Then at last they understood that he wasn't
speaking about the yeast in bread, but about the deceptive teaching of
the Pharisees and Sadducees.*

*When Jesus came to the region of Caesarea Philippi, he asked his
disciples, "Who do people say that the Son of Man is?"*

*"Well," they replied, "some say John the Baptist, some say Elijah,
and others say Jeremiah or one of the other prophets."*

Then he asked them, "But who do you say I am?"

Simon Peter answered, "You are the Messiah, the Son of the living

God."

Jesus replied, "You are blessed, Simon son of John, because my Father in heaven has revealed this to you. You did not learn this from any human being. Now I say to you that you are Peter (which means 'rock'), and upon this rock I will build my church, and all the powers of hell will not conquer it. And I will give you the keys of the Kingdom of Heaven. Whatever you forbid on earth will be forbidden in heaven, and whatever you permit on earth will be permitted in heaven." Then he sternly warned the disciples not to tell anyone that he was the Messiah. (NLT)

The danger that Jesus warns His disciples of in verse 6 is "the leaven of... the doctrine of the Pharisees and Sadducees". This issue is serious enough for Him to bluntly judge these religious elite *"hypocrites"* and to tell the disciples to be on their guard to avoid their doctrine. He is not telling the disciples to avoid contact with Pharisees or Sadducees but exposes an earmark of "bad doctrine." When He says *"take heed and beware,"* He is saying "pay attention", "be aware" of their teaching and how what they teach infects their following. Don't be afraid of checking out doctrines that are being taught. Find out what they are really based on and what they produce.

DOCTRINE:

Instruction or what is taught, especially a summarized body of respected teaching.

EARMARK OF "BAD DOCTRINE":

"Show us a sign." That may seem to be only the superficial circus-hunters, but there's more to it. It's circus hunting for the purpose of a special kind of validation – for Jesus to prove Himself and His power. One of the main points here is that their request is superficial, which illustrates where these guys were living and that they didn't actually want to validate Jesus' authority. They wanted to debunk it, especially if He meant to dethrone them as the ones in control over the spiritual identity of Israel.

In verse 13 Jesus asks the disciples, *"Who do people say I am?"* Based on natural impressions and rumor, people were coming up with many opinions about who Jesus might be. Then in verse 15 He asks the disciples, *"So, who do you say I am?"* To which Peter answers, *"You are the Messiah, the Son of the Living God."* Jesus, spotlighting the contrast between calculations using natural impression (real or rumored) and divine revelation, responds, *"Flesh and blood (superficial evidence) has not revealed this to you, but My Father who is in heaven."*

Speaking of revelation, there certainly is an abundance of people who say that God told them something. Is there any verification for that? It seems as though these pious men grilling Jesus had come up with some sort of formula or doctrine to judge by. Was it a good one or a bad one? We can detect from what Jesus says that it was definitely *not* a good one.

How bad is their doctrine? Jesus answers that question, *"A wicked and adulterous generation seeks after a sign."* Jesus is the master wordsmith. Those words were chosen very specifically. Look closely to register what He actually said and what the listeners heard...

In the Old Testament
Wicked: bad, *evil*, good for nothing
(This word was used to describe Noah's generation and people of Sodom.)
Adulterous: to commit adultery, common, physically and spiritually

In the New Testament
Wicked: more evil, hurtful evil; anguish, starving; worthless, depravity, lawless, criminal
Adulterous: an adulteress, a (male) paramour
Seeks: to search for; to **crave**

These words seem to point to people completely outside the Kingdom of God – yes? But wait. He's saying this to the religious elite, the highest in the Kingdom (according to their formula). How can this be? It seems clear that religious or not, humans are very weak when it comes to resisting the *"**leaven**,"* hypocrisy of the world's mind-set. The craving for sensational signs as well as sensual gratification also seems to be a natural earmark of that kind of philosophy.

What's so bad about wanting signs and miracles? For one thing, they can be falsified, especially in our show business culture, and therefore, over time, will destroy any true sense of discernment. Another related danger is that by looking for signs we're likely to miss what God is actually doing and wants us to see. How do we know what to look for? Do we dictate to God how He shows Himself to us? Do we set the guidelines for His dealings with us and how His Spirit works? The typical answer usually given is, "We don't predict what's going to happen the Holy Spirit just leads!" Oh really? So why is it that after weeks or years He's still only doing the exact same things? Who's the leader now?

I've actually been in churches where pastors who, after seeing a real outpouring of the Holy Spirit some weeks before, try to reproduce that in every service since, by singing the same song or saying the same phrases they think triggered it the first time. They loudly proclaim, "A great outpouring is happening at our church!" The poor musicians sing the song a few times because the pastor insists. Then when "the move" doesn't happen, he rushes to the microphone and shouts, "Sing that song again!" That is just one embarrassing example of our creativity in "helping the Holy Spirit." My point is this: We look where we want to look. We expect what happened before or what we heard has happened. And when we do, we are robbed and we rob other people. We don't hear the voice of God calling us to repentance and intimacy. We are not being washed by the Living Water of His Word for that moment. Even if there were a cloudburst of the pure water of the Word, we wouldn't notice. It just rolls off like water on a duck's back. All the while we defend what occurs as fresh and new. Jesus says that this mentality is found in a *"wicked and adulterous generation"* caught up in the gratification of its own impulse and whim, consuming every opportunity on the appetite of their *"flesh and blood"* (see Matt 16:15-17 AMP).

THE ALTERNATIVE:

Genuine God-breathed revelation which comes exclusively from actual whole-soul immersion in all that God is, along with absolute surrender to all He reveals through His nature and His indwelling Holy Spirit. That is the ROCK on which the church is built. That is the standard for judging whether the teaching or doctrine is good or bad.

While we openly live out His disposition in every situation, conversation and test, Jesus surely is able and faithful to equip His disciples to discern between the two. And that equipment is in place when He and the Father send the Other to plug it in and put it to work, giving us and those He touches through our lives, a clear choice. He destroys the devil's delusion that humility is the opposite of powerful and to succeed we must dominate by any means. The question is: *Do we discern* the difference between them? If we do, then we must walk openly in that knowledge, humbly and without apology, modeling what loyalty to Jesus and true dependency on His Spirit look like. If we realize we are not discerning, then with all our might we must completely turn from our self-dependency and personal sovereignty, and refuse the temptation to try to fabricate the Power of the Spirit. We cannot afford to yield to our delusion of power and use it to manipulate people. If we become aware that we have the power to manipulate people, we need to be very afraid. The immediate action in that instance should be to turn and run hard into Jesus. Learn His ways and practice His disposition in our skin. We must willfully determine not to compromise with the temptations of the devil to satisfy his craving for domination, by using our skin to do it. We will stand before God's throne and be exposed before *all* of God's people.

It is time we stand for nothing but the real thing. The real thing always builds every believer up for the discovery of their own work of ministry. There's no joy like participating with God's own Spirit as He touches His children and pours His life through us. We are all called to eternal life for the human connection to His agenda in those He gives us to. Let's get real and stick with it!

Chapter Twenty Two

SURPRISE, SURPRISE!
Matthew 16:21-28

From then on Jesus began to tell his disciples plainly that it was necessary for him to go to Jerusalem, and that he would suffer many terrible things at the hands of the elders, the leading priests, and the teachers of religious law. He would be killed, but on the third day he would be raised from the dead.

But Peter took him aside and began to reprimand him for saying such things. "Heaven forbid, Lord," he said. "This will never happen to you!"

Jesus turned to Peter and said, "Get away from me, Satan! You are a dangerous trap to me. You are seeing things merely from a human point of view, not from God's."

Then Jesus said to his disciples, "If any of you wants to be my follower, you must turn from your selfish ways, take up your cross, and follow me. If you try to hang on to your life, you will lose it. But if you give up your life for my sake, you will save it. And what do you benefit if you gain the whole world but lose your own soul? Is anything worth more than your soul? For the Son of Man will come with his angels in the glory of his Father and will judge all people according to their deeds. And I tell you the truth, some standing here right now will not die before they see the Son of Man coming in his Kingdom." (NLT)

Jesus was now saying very clearly that He *"must go to Jerusalem, and suffer many things from the elders and chief priests and scribes, and be killed, and be raised the third day."* When what He was saying actually sank in, Peter pulls Him aside and very heroically says, "That is not going to happen to You!" Jesus spins around and says for all ears, *"Get behind Me, Satan!"*

Wow! We have just heard Jesus say to Peter that his faith in Him as the Messiah was the rock on which the church would be built upon. And now He's turning His back on Peter and saying *"Get behind Me, Satan!"* What's happening?

This is a very stark illustration of how far and how quickly we, very human Christians, can swerve out of control and sometimes crash head-on into an immovable God and not even see it coming! Quickly taking up a cause, any cause, is very dangerous, especially if it is based in an emotional issue. If not dangerous to our eternal destiny, it is definitely dangerous to our pride. Just think of how this whiplash-turn affected an emotionally driven and deeply vulnerable Peter.

Our clear goal is to be alive with the brand name "LIFE" without worrying that we might rock the Christendom boat. "If anyone desires to come after Me, let him deny himself, and take up his cross. That's how following Me is done (my paraphrase)." What I desire above all things is to see His welcoming smile and to hear Him say, *"Well done, good and faithful servant"* (see Matt 25:21). The question is, am I doing what He says?

This discourse holds a powerful encouragement to those who find it difficult at times to distinguish any hard, clear border between right and wrong; what is from God and what is not. It is obvious in this scene that Jesus sees the line very clearly and is determined that we should see it too. For Peter, He was right there in the flesh. For us, Jesus has come to dwell in our hearts and He is constantly available for us to lean on and learn from. That is what *"deny himself"* means: constant verification and deferment to Jesus' view and purpose.

That is not just a "have church" kind of thing. Rather, it is "Church", as in *"your body – the Temple of the Holy Spirit"* kind of thing (see 1Cor 6:19-20). Those inspirational moments in church meetings are supposed to be bringing us to an awareness of the Holy Spirit's function day after day in every situation and process of our daily relationships. *"Lo, I am with you always,"* Jesus says. And, *"I'll never leave you nor forsake you."* When we gather, we do so to reveal and remind each other that Jesus is there and challenge each other to let Him rule. When the Church gathers, whether it be with 2 or 2,000, it is to be an environment in which we can practice surrendering darkened areas of our hearts to His rulership, without regard to attempts of exploitation and manipulation by opportunistic wolves – especially by our own heart.

The line between truth and deception gets clearer once we get the message Jesus gave Peter, *"You are not concerned with the things of God, but the things of men!"* That should be the most surprising and embarrassing discovery for a Christian, though it is almost surely the most common. Anytime we are calculating solely on the data we have between our ears, or fed our emotions, we are not able to see that line any more, because we are striving so hard to change the *things* that seem, to us, to be out of whack, in order to make them work the way we think they should. Those *things* are the very *things* that God has designed to discipline and train us, if we will only humble ourselves before Him and behold the continuity of the undefeated Creator of all *things*.

That is how striving comes into the picture. There is a very deep, powerful longing inside of us that poses itself as complete and sufficient. It seems admirable at first glimpse, even a signal of intentional integrity. But the illusions of being self-complete and self-sufficient avoid help from anyone else and is lust for personal sovereignty [lust: must have it now]. That is *the* plague inflicted on the whole human race. There's another way to say it – Oswald Chambers said it perfectly in his definition of sin, "My claim, to my right, to myself." That appetite surfaces and begins to forcefully defend its perceived territory very early in our lives, long before we have any power to reject it. Parents are solely responsible for instilling any controls on that craving, and we are all familiar with the destruction that happens if they do not believe that is their job.

This "plague" pits us against everything that threatens our right to defend our personal sovereignty. That means we are going to be at odds with everything around us. Every suggestion or, correction, builds another layer of bitterness and rage against either the person, the preacher's interpretation of a Bible verse, or any situation that forces us to conclude that things around us are just crazy enough to insult the way we see them. Pride is a bulldozer and would rather see us dead than let us ask for help or even consider that our vindictive reaction to everything that happens rejects the fact that every one of those threats to our sovereignty is a God-designed chance to break loose and mature beyond the view of a two-year-old child. As adults, pride reduces us to distempered animals. That is exactly why Jesus lived a pure life in spite of every corrupting force and surrendered His life on the cross. He has given *us* the prerogative to "*Submit to God. Resist the devil, and he will run away from you*" (James 4:7 CJB), so we can see the domination of the "*father of all liars*" evicted from our broken human heart.

MAKE IT PERSONAL

Is it ever too late and too much work to see that transformation take place? Some person may come to mind for whom this seems impossible. Maybe it's you. BUT – it wasn't too late for Abram or Noah or Job or Jacob or Joseph or Moses or Samuel or David or Isaiah or Jeremiah or Gideon or Samson or Nehemiah or Esther or Matthew, John, James, Peter, not even for the thief on the cross next to Jesus! The only people who are truly hopeless are the ones who refuse to deny themselves the right to sit on the throne of their own hearts.

Here are a couple of examples of that obstinacy: the other thief and Judas. And how about the entire population of the world before the flood (except one family who built a ship), or Lucifer himself? Death is a bitter pill for those who spend their last breath singing "I DID IT MY WAY". An admirable sounding attitude if your idea of success is to dominate a pack of rats, taking whatever and whoever can be taken. More triumphantly however, is the fact that there is a God in heaven who SO LOVED that He sent His Son to defeat Lucifer's demonic rebellion and save those who had been caught in its net, His most highly treasured creation – His children – us.

Chapter Twenty Three

SEE JESUS IN HIS KINGDOM?
Matthew 17:1-13

*S*ix *days later Jesus took Peter and the two brothers, James and John, and led them up a high mountain to be alone. As the men watched, Jesus' appearance was transformed so that his face shone like the sun, and his clothes became as white as light. Suddenly, Moses and Elijah appeared and began talking with Jesus.*

Peter exclaimed, "Lord, it's wonderful for us to be here! If you want, I'll make three shelters as memorials—one for you, one for Moses, and one for Elijah."

But even as he spoke, a bright cloud overshadowed them, and a voice from the cloud said, "This is my dearly loved Son, who brings me great joy. Listen to him." The disciples were terrified and fell face down on the ground.

Then Jesus came over and touched them. "Get up," he said. "Don't be afraid." And when they looked up, Moses and Elijah were gone, and they saw only Jesus. As they went back down the mountain, Jesus commanded them, "Don't tell anyone what you have seen until the Son of Man has been raised from the dead."

Then his disciples asked him, "Why do the teachers of religious law insist that Elijah must return before the Messiah comes?"

Jesus replied, "Elijah is indeed coming first to get everything ready. But I tell you, Elijah has already come, but he wasn't recognized, and they chose to abuse him. And in the same way they will also make the Son of Man suffer." Then the disciples realized he was talking about John the Baptist. (NLT)

A FEW OBSERVATIONS:

1) Why Matthew points out that this episode happened "*6 days*" later is interesting. Luke says it was "*8 days*" later. Later than what? Jesus and team were known to take leisure time in Caesarea Philippi. It

could be that the confrontations that had just happened there needed that much time to sink in. Think Jesus might have needed to chill for a week just to keep from completely short-circuiting Peter's brain? If that does not seem plausible, then, we have to settle on the differing days to be the result of Matt and Luke getting their data separately from two different disciples.

2) Peter, James and John seemed to be preferred by Jesus as His closest companions. I'm sure this assumption should include at least a glance at what Paul points out, "the dishonorable members of the body need the most attention." Check out 1Corinthians 12:23-24. No, I'm not saying they were dishonorable, but it bears consideration that these three were the loud, impulsive guys in the group and whatever they got would naturally be broadcast to everyone. Besides, I'm sure Jesus saw the need to keep a close eye on them! After all, these are the same James and John (*the Sons of Thunder*) who wanted to call in an airstrike on one of the Samaritan villages that didn't welcome them.

3) *"Jesus led them."* Led here, is *anaphero,* which actually means *carry.* Two things we can be sure of – He knew where He was going, and He was looking forward to the talk with Moses and Elijah. Actually blowing the three disciples' minds must have been an entertaining bonus.

4) *"Up on a high mountain."* Historic and geographic insight: Tradition has it [Origen in the 3rd Century, St. Cyril and St. Jerome in the 4th Century and in the 5th Century it is mentioned by Transitus Beatae Mariae Virginis] that Mt Tabor is the "mount of transfiguration." In fact, a Franciscan Monastery was completed in 1924 on the ruins of a 5th Century Byzantine church there. Also on top of Mt Tabor there is a 12th Century church of the Crusader Kingdom. There's also a Greek Orthodox Monastery there. So faithful religious zealots have actually done what Peter wanted to do and built the shrines he suggested should be built, but more than likely, on the wrong hill; and I do mean hill. Mt Tabor rises 1,886 feet above sea level. Not exactly a mountain, nor is it lofty, but much easier for pilgrims to get up to. Mt Hermon rises 9,232 feet, a *high mountain*, indeed. Another important point in favor of Hermon being the mountain of Matt 17:1 is that Jesus and His disciples had just spent 6-8 days in Caesarea Philippi, which is up around Upper Galilee, close to Mt Hermon.

"His clothes became as white as light." Jesus had just said in 16:28, *"There are those here who will not taste death before they see the kingdom of God come in [its] power"* (AMPC). Later, Jesus would use that vivid picture in John's memory. In Revelation 3:5 he relates

Jesus' words, *"He who overcomes shall be clothed in white garments,"* and v18, *"I counsel you to buy from Me gold refined in the fire, that you may be rich; and white garments, that you may be clothed."* It is the glory of God that His powerful nature be seen in "earthen" vessels.

"Then Peter answered." Let's stop right there. When Peter saw and heard Moses and Elijah talking to Jesus, he *had* to say something. This must have been a common reflex with Peter – answering, that is; reacting, feeling obligated or compelled to speak even though nothing could be more inappropriate. Some people's emotions overcome their brains, which are hot-wired to their lips. To paraphrase an old proverb: Words that force themselves through carnal lips are usually not worth the breath.

> Here is an apropos quote from the transformative prayer in AW Tozer's book, THE KNOWLEDGE OF THE HOLY which gives the other, more beautiful, side of this coin: "Lord, how great is our dilemma! In Thy Presence silence best becomes us, but love inflames our hearts and constrains us to speak. Were we to hold our peace the stones would cry out; yet if we speak, what shall we say? Teach us to know that we cannot know, for the things of God knoweth no man, but the Spirit of God. Let faith support us where reason fails, and we shall think because we believe, not in order that we may believe."

I am part Chickasaw Indian and have heard their comments about the contrast in this particular area between them and the white man. Indian men can sit for days in a lodge together and never feel compelled to say a word. A white man would go crazy. He has to have some kind of auditory stimulus, perhaps to be reminded he's alive or to be sure he's okay. He has to say something no matter how mindless it might be. He just doesn't know how to be still. Yet, to learn to be still seems an integral requirement in this Way of Eternal Life.

Eternal Life is *"to know the only true God and the One He sent"* (John 17:3), and knowing is available to those who will be still. *"Be still, and know that I am God"* (Ps 46:10).

"While Peter was still talking." This is a good wake up call to those who question whether God knows what they are thinking or hears what they say. Before Peter even finishes what he was saying, God responds. A bright cloud enveloped them, GOD speaks out loud and when they heard His voice they hit the ground, face in the dirt, *"greatly afraid"*.

In our vernacular today what He said would sound something like, "Seriously? This is MY SON! In the presence of His voice and His wisdom, silence best befits you. Keep your focus on Him, and instead of needing to hear your own voice, listen to Him!"

Jesus came over and touched them. He said, *"Come on, get up. Don't be afraid."* Do those words sound familiar? This must be one of Jesus' most common tasks with humans. I guess if He were pressed by time He would get real tired of saying that. He must have to say it more than a million times a day with all the fearful, worrying Christians in this world.

Just before they were thrown to the ground, the disciples were seeing Moses, Elijah, Jesus and each other. They were hearing all those voices, not to mention God's! When they looked up, they saw and heard Jesus ONLY. Moses represented the LAW, and Elijah represented the PROPHETS. This is a beautiful picture of the personal consolidation of God's expression and authority in His Son, Jesus. Suddenly Jesus was all they saw and all they heard.

Think they wouldn't be listening after that? I don't think they had a problem focusing anymore. I also think that their faith was expanded to the point that they would *"have the ears to hear"* whatever they heard Jesus say. Up to that point their ears had been filtering what Jesus said through their own points of view. It seems probable that at this point they had a little more sensible evaluation of their opinions. So I'm sure they were quite eager to comply with, *"Don't tell anyone about this until I'm raised from the dead."* I can just hear their response, "You bet!"

On the way down from the mountain, they began to process what they had seen, and the question arises, "So what are the scribes talking about when they say Elijah has to come first [before the Messiah]?" This was one more confirmation that they knew who Jesus was speaking to. But they were having trouble putting together what they had seen with the accepted interpretation of Scripture. (Ever notice how God is always clarifying Himself?) They didn't have pictures of Moses or Elijah, so they didn't recognize them by sight. It is more likely that they heard the three of them greeting each other and listened closely to what they were saying. They had obviously told Luke because he records that they were talking about Jesus' death.

Jesus explains to them that Elijah *did* come first. This brings up an interesting line of thought. Was John somehow an incarnation of Elijah? We know that Elijah had not experienced death yet and Scripture is clear on the subject of death; *"...it is appointed for [all] men once to die"* (Hebrews 9:27 AMPC). Was Elijah preserved alive for his one death, till he was sent in John the Baptist? If so, now Moses and Elijah both had died, and that's what they were talking with Jesus about. This is completely out of my league, but Matthew does say, *"The disciples understood that He spoke to them of John the Baptist."*

CONCLUSION OF THE MATTER

This passage doesn't indicate that Jesus said anything to Peter, James or John after those last words of Matthew 16, *"...see the kingdom of God come in [its] power,"* until after God had spoken to them. When they were flat on their faces and unable to breathe, He says, *"Get up. Don't be afraid"* (Matt 17:7). I believe that God is speaking to us. What He shows us is beyond our imaginations. Some of His words are harsh and cutting, especially to our self-absorbed sensitivities.

It would be good to remember that God does not have to speak to us at all. He would get rid of a lot of grief if He would just discard us. But He is our Father, and it is love that motivates Him to speak to us. We seem to think that the role of a father is somehow to nurture without any confrontation or hands-on training. That discards a large chunk of God's Book which deals extensively with the subject as well as its consequences. God's way of parenting is not a popularity contest but a trust and character building contest to counter what is bound up in our hearts when we are born. Discarding God's love and training for children can easily produce a young man or woman with only themselves to look to and no solid place to stand – one of the most direct ploys of the enemy of their souls.

Truth is not optional or timid, nor is it ambiguous. Truth seems anything BUT nurturing, until the one in danger comes into its sure refuge. Truth-spoken-in-love does not equal truth-spoken-lovingly. The Bible does not say that God is loving, which is based in emotion. It establishes that God *is* love, which is self-sacrificial, responsible determination. Everything He speaks to us is Truth in love, in Spirit and in Life. What He says is ultimate reality in the world we can see, as well as in the world we can not see. We can not afford to let any area of our life be an entrance for Satan to infest us with vindictive self-pity because of the way God speaks to us, through circumstances, other people or directly through His Word. Maturity and character is our responsibility by obedient adjustment to the training course He has created for us to complete trust in His promises and personal revelation of His nature through His Son. Any self focused worship or sovereignty is demonic and is a breech that must be closed up before our grudge against God causes someone else to take offense at Him. There is not a living soul who did not initially feel mistreated when a disciplinary action was administered by a parent who loved enough to draw a clear line. Many of us have yet to grow out of that and, until we do, we are in danger of slandering God.

God is love and His love has been shed abroad in us. He will speak to and through us in the precise way required to clearly get His point across. For hardheads, that means it will sometimes have to cut deep and disrupt everything we think. Is that okay with us? Now, hear Jesus say, "Come on. Get up. Don't be afraid. Don't tell anyone about this until I am fully alive in this issue and my Truth has become yours. The world does not know me and will do what they wish with Me, but you are different. You are Mine. You will know Me and that will make you My light to the world" (see Matt 17:7-9).

Chapter Twenty Four

GLORIFY GOD? ME?
Matthew 17:14-27

*A*t the foot of the mountain, a large crowd was waiting for them. A man came and knelt before Jesus and said, "Lord, have mercy on my son. He has seizures and suffers terribly. He often falls into the fire or into the water. So I brought him to your disciples, but they couldn't heal him."

Jesus said, "You faithless and corrupt people! How long must I be with you? How long must I put up with you? Bring the boy here to me." Then Jesus rebuked the demon in the boy, and it left him. From that moment the boy was well.

Afterward the disciples asked Jesus privately, "Why couldn't we cast out that demon?"

He answered, "Because of your little faith [your lack of trust and confidence in the power of God]; for I assure you and most solemnly say to you, if you have [living] faith the size of a mustard seed, you will say to this mountain, 'Move from here to there,' and [if it is God's will] it would move; and nothing will be impossible for you." [later mss say, "But this kind of demon does not go out except by prayer and fasting."] (AMP)

After they gathered again in Galilee, Jesus told them, "The Son of Man is going to be betrayed into the hands of his enemies. He will be killed, but on the third day he will be raised from the dead." And the disciples were filled with grief.

On their arrival in Capernaum, the collectors of the Temple tax came to Peter and asked him, "Doesn't your teacher pay the Temple tax?"

"Yes, he does," Peter replied. Then he went into the house.

But before he had a chance to speak, Jesus asked him, "What do you think, Peter? Do kings tax their own people or the people they have conquered?"

"They tax the people they have conquered," Peter replied.

"Well, then," Jesus said, "the citizens are free! However, we don't want to offend them, so go down to the lake and throw in a line. Open the mouth of the first fish you catch, and you will find a large silver coin. Take it and pay the tax for both of us." (NLT)

In Matthew 17:1-13 the glory of the beloved Son of God is revealed, seen by humans in the connection to His death. Luke 9:31 reveals that He was talking to Moses and Elijah *"of His decease which He was about to accomplish at Jerusalem."*

Now Matthew 17:14-27 shows a subtle but powerful illustration of the "how-to" so that His glory would shine through His disciples as well.

As you read through these verses notice the sequence:

• An epileptic boy is dominated by the terrestrial elements, the phases of the moon and earth-bound spirits.

• This kind only comes out by prayer with fasting – the actions required: cast away dominance by the flesh and the world and establish submission to the dominance of the Holy Spirit of God.

• Submission to death! This might seem to be only slipped in here, but notice: This is what Jesus is talking about at that time, in that place, so it must be a crucial point in the sequence.

• The glory of God, Divine order, is re-established by a coin in a fish's mouth! That was a mind-boggling proof that Jesus, the Messiah, indeed had power over the elements of nature.

Did Jesus blow Peter's mind? Does Jesus blow our minds? Can we see the depth of the installation that Jesus is accomplishing in Peter? He was preparing ground deep inside Peter and the others that would be full of the nutrients necessary for the harvest of souls when the time was right. They would discover that their connection to, and dependency on Him, would be something completely outside their comprehension.

Could it be that this "ground" of deep preparation that Jesus was plowing and planting in the disciples' lives has gone fallow and unproductive through the years of man's help establishing the church? Take an honest look at our life in Christ. Is it possible that we are fueling our personal and corporal Christianity with less than the deep transformation and resurrection that only the Spirit of God can accomplish or even understand? Jesus' words were astonishing, wall-crushing, wise and powerful, but they were just words until the Spirit was waited upon; until He installed in those disciples His own abiding

Presence to will and to do His good pleasure.

We are ravenously swallowing the words, the teachings, even the doctrines and theology. That can be very satisfying, as well as consuming our time and energies to the point that we feel as though we are fulfilling the purposes of God. If the hearing, the study, and the preaching does not take us beyond the learning of new concepts and the gathering of information, we have not attained to the worship of the simplest child who talks to Jesus and has Him living in their heart.

The question is, have we waited on the Holy Spirit to transform us into the incarnation of His words? Are Jesus' words the expression of our life? After Jesus had spoken all the words and given all the instruction, He said to the disciples, *"... when He, the Spirit of truth, has come, He will guide you into all truth"* (John 16:13).

SOUL SEARCH

Do you hunger as I do that the Glory of God would shine through us? That we could be one with Him and that His order would be established in us? That He could destroy the works and strongholds of the devil in our own hearts and homes as well as in the lives of those we come in contact with?

If you do, then no earthly power has the authority to keep you from it. No cost or effort in this world's terms is too great to exchange for the glory of God. Glory = Him being seen, heard, fellowshipped with in this physical world by the agency of His yielded mortal body-parts, anytime and anywhere we are. That's why we are there, why He has orchestrated everything to make it so.

Chapter Twenty Five

WHO THEN?
Matthew 18:1-6

*A*bout that time the disciples came to Jesus and asked, "Who is greatest in the Kingdom of Heaven?" Jesus called a little child to him and put the child among them. Then he said, "I tell you the truth, unless you turn from your sins and become like little children, you will never get into the Kingdom of Heaven. So anyone who becomes as humble as this little child is the greatest in the Kingdom of Heaven.

"And anyone who welcomes a little child like this on my behalf is welcoming me. But if you cause one of these little ones who trusts in me to fall into sin, it would be better for you to have a large millstone tied around your neck and be drowned in the depths of the sea." (NLT)

The question of "who is greatest" then, may be because of what Peter had just done previously. I don't know, but isn't that the most common debate among the disciples, "Who is the greatest?" And when we ask it, aren't we usually a bit puzzled because Jesus doesn't seem to answer the question? Before talking about what makes us great, He takes first things first and talks about the requirement for merely qualifying for the competition.

The operative words are *"unless you are converted and become..."* and *"whoever humbles himself..."* It is clear that the transformation comes because we are "converted" and become as little children by humbling ourselves. Converted, brings to mind a very specific picture.

If we travel internationally we have to carry a "power converter" to be able to use our electrical appliances. Not only is the plug different, the power is different. AC, DC, 100 volt, 110 volt, 220 volt, 50 cycles, 60 cycles, etc. The point is that the appliance we want to use must be converted to match the power we plug it into, and that takes another totally separate device. If not for this device, the result can be very surprising and usually very destructive, not to mention smelly. Sometimes I feel it would be helpful if the results were more obvious when we try to plug into the kingdom of God without being converted. No matter what you do about the burning smell, it just can't be done.

There's only one way to plug in. Our converter is Jesus. Whatever we do, we must do by Him, His way, if we expect it to be in sync enough with eternity to have eternal value in the context of His purposes. We can't manufacture the converter or do His work, but it is clear that plugging in and actually entering the kingdom of Heaven takes some effort and determination on our part. We must see that "entering into the kingdom of Heaven" means the domain of Heaven, the rulership of Jesus. *"In the kingdom"* means, our body is now annexed as territory under Jesus' dominion. Like a ship at sea, it is a floating part of its home country which has sent it out on mission.

Entry into the kingdom of Heaven is accomplished by the same action as becoming the greatest in that kingdom. Just as running fast is the way we get into a race - it is also how we win that race. Paul called this life a race. If we want to run a race we must first qualify by running – fast enough. Once we are in the race, Paul says we must run to win. We win by the same means as we qualify. We run – fast enough.

We may have used all the power we possessed to just qualify; but once qualified, we must train and learn how to increase and focus our strength so we can run, not just fast enough, but the fastest. Effort must be exerted, and loyalty and sacrifice for the goal must become all consuming. No cost is too great. Winning is all there is. The power is coming to the converter but the determination and effort must be ours, to allow the power to flow through at full output.

"Be converted and BECOME..." Become what? Become as a little child. How? There's only one way – *"Therefore whoever humbles himself as this little child is the greatest in the kingdom of heaven."* *"Humbles himself AS THIS little child."* Look at the child. He has just been called over by Jesus. Then Jesus *"set him in the midst of them."* Did the child know what was going on or why Jesus called him or put him in the middle of these men? Of course not. He just came when Jesus called and was willing to be put into any position Jesus would desire.

The child is: surprised, without fearful unwillingness; moved, without need of gaining personal control; raptured in the sound of the Shepherd's call; and giggling with glee at yielding to His strong hand – His purpose. That is the greatest! And if the greatest in the kingdom of Heaven, then the greatest in all kingdoms.

Does a child have to exert effort to be as a child? No; but a man does. We are obviously not talking about being childish. We are talking about being willing to have no identity except Jesus... being Jesus-with-skin-on in each conversation, each challenge and response, each point of identification. We are not "trying" to be like Jesus or "trying" to *Do-What-Jesus-Would-Do*. Why do that when we are humbled as that child and the real Jesus can do whatever He wants through us any time He wants? Does it sound like arrogance to say that to receive one of us is to receive Jesus? It is, unless we're plugged in, converted and turned fully on. Besides, we didn't say it. He did. And we are simply but completely in Him.

Humble is a word that some have said includes a correct and honest view of one's self. That has sent millions of people on a quest to "know themselves". However, the correct view of self is hardly a glance, neither demeaning nor defending self. Jesus' way has nothing to do with the quest for "self realization." Just as our eastern and pagan friends have said, "There is a blissful nothingness at the end of the realization of self." Yes! I have been there. There is nothingness alright, but it is definitely not blissful!

So, we are in a humility-race? Yes! Let's outdo each other in allowing Jesus to do acts of kindness and sacrificing Himself in our joyful surrender to Him for those we have been put with and given to. Run to win! Not only does that qualify us, but it marks us as **winner**.

Chapter Twenty Six

HUMILITY
Matthew 18:1-20

*A*bout that time the disciples came to Jesus and asked, "Who is greatest in the Kingdom of Heaven?" Jesus called a little child to him and put the child among them. Then he said, "I tell you the truth, unless you turn from your sins* and become like little children, you will never get into the Kingdom of Heaven. So anyone who becomes as humble as this little child is the greatest in the Kingdom of Heaven.

"And anyone who welcomes a little child like this on my behalf is welcoming me. But if you cause one of these little ones who trusts in me to fall into sin, it would be better for you to have a large millstone tied around your neck and be drowned in the depths of the sea. What sorrow awaits the world, because it tempts people to sin. Temptations are inevitable, but what sorrow awaits the person who does the tempting. So if your hand or foot causes you to sin, cut it off and throw it away. It's better to enter eternal life with only one hand or one foot than to be thrown into eternal fire with both of your hands and feet. And if your eye causes you to sin, gouge it out and throw it away. It's better to enter eternal life with only one eye than to have two eyes and be thrown into the fire of hell.

"Beware that you don't look down on any of these little ones. For I tell you that in heaven their angels are always in the presence of my heavenly Father.

"If a man has a hundred sheep and one of them wanders away, what will he do? Won't he leave the ninety-nine others on the hills and go out to search for the one that is lost? And if he finds it, I tell you the truth, he will rejoice over it more than over the ninety-nine that didn't wander away! In the same way, it is not my heavenly Father's will that even one of these little ones should perish.

"If another believer sins* against you, go privately and point out the offense. *If the other person listens and confesses it, you have won that person back. But if you are unsuccessful, take one or two others with you and go back again, so that everything you say may be confirmed by two or three witnesses. If the person still refuses to listen, take your case to the church. Then if he or she won't accept the church's decision, treat that person as a pagan or a corrupt tax collector. I tell you the truth, whatever you forbid on earth will be forbidden in heaven, and whatever you permit on earth will be permitted in heaven.*

"I also tell you this: If two of you agree here on earth concerning anything you ask, my Father in heaven will do it for you. For where two or three gather together as my followers, I am there among them." (NLT)

*sins = my autonomous claims to my right to my independent significance.

In the last chapter, the operative words were *"converted and become."*

Transformation comes because we are *"converted"* and we *"become"* as a child by humbling ourselves.

Let's look at the whole section, verses 1-20, with our eye on *"whoever humbles himself."* How does that look?

Humility includes a correct, honest view of self. If we think about just that challenge for a few moments, to actually come to a correct and practical perception of our self, I'm pretty sure we will finally conclude that coming up with that on our own is impossible. I've known people who come close, but there's only one way to get there. Start from the Cornerstone, Jesus, placing Him at the base on which we can even start to build any understanding of what those words really mean ... real, humble, honest and wise.

The first thing we are forced to acknowledge is that His thoughts are different from ours and that He has come to live in us so that through our yielded body and disposition He can do His work, though I may not have a clue what He is doing. My ideas, perceptions and expectations are challenged and must be laid aside, sacrificed to give way to His ideas, perceptions and expectations. Our perception and thoughts cannot possibly be a base for anything completely real and worthy of trust. By turning to Jesus and asking for His wisdom and insight, we open up the door that activates His promise to reveal Himself to those who love Him [*"who do what I say"*]. That's the picture He gives by standing the child there in the middle of them. Then He demands, "As an adult, you have the power to decide what you do. Decide to become as this child, ready to be a student. Humble yourself and learn to serve My interests toward those around you."

The disciples are looking at the child, listening to what Jesus is saying. They go from being rebuked for their competitive, self-promoting attitudes to being given a very powerful incentive to carry out His command to *"humble yourself."*

What must have gone through the minds of Peter, James and John as Jesus described what would be in store for anyone who caused one of these little ones to be kept from coming to Him? "You can't stop God's children from having troubles in this world. But you'd better not be the one who causes it! Being strapped to a millstone and thrown into the sea would be better than what will happen to you."

Big contrast, isn't it? Either become the *"greatest in the Kingdom"* by humbling ourselves – OR – by pushing our way around to assert our rights in which case we will surely, in due time, wish we were but thrown in the river wearing cement boots! Overly dramatic? I don't think Jesus would agree. Why do I think that? Because He immediately describes what we should do if we suddenly discover that a part of our nature is actually defying this command. The action is to be swift and violent or lose our place in the Kingdom.

The action we are to take to stop ourselves from dealing wrongly with these *"little ones"* is based on insight into God's thoughts about a child who goes astray. Allow me to paraphrase what Jesus says: "God does not want any of His kids to be led astray and perish. He'll leave the rest and go after that kid and when He gets back, there's going to be hell to pay for the one who is responsible. So, if your brother does something against you, go and tell him. Don't just cut him off and start telling people what he did. Go give him a chance to hear your insight so your relationship can be restored. Don't be afraid. If you can get together, I'll be right there with you. Only take it beyond the two of you if he won't listen. You need 2 witnesses in that case. Only then does it become a public matter. If the two of you are able to bind that thing up, then it's bound in heaven. But if you do all you can do and just can't patch it up, then the relationship is broken, here and in heaven."

Can you sense the great pain of our Creator when relationship is broken? He is more serious about that than we are. We can't be flippant about our dealings with the people to whom God connects us. Don't easily write someone off and justify it with some reference to a Biblical rule that was broken. Resist the self-deifying spirit of the antichrist. Hear the Father's heart: *"Restore such a brother."* They've had enough troubles without us adding to them. "Reconcile the broken relationship." Repent of the unyielding defense of our claim to our own right to be the right one. Look for a reason to truly be humble and say, "I'm sorry. Please, forgive me." Those words are the best medicine for the woes of this life. Restore. Reconcile. Love. A true friend is a treasure, loyal, truthful and humble (generous, practical realism).

"Where two or three of my followers are gathered together, I am there." If we gather in His name [in everything His name means to each one] He rises in the middle of that interaction and feeds us on the multiplicity of who He is in each of us and reveals the orchestration of our lives and inseparable relationships as parts of His own flesh and blood Body, His physical presence in the spot we stand on. He reveals in us His heart, humility, honesty and wisdom, active in the conversation we engage in, and in His intercession in which He graciously invites us to join Him.

Chapter Twenty Seven

ACCOUNTING vs. GOD'S WAYS
Matthew 18:21-35

*T*hen Peter came to him and asked, "Lord, how often should I forgive someone who sins against me? Seven times?"

"No, not seven times," Jesus replied, "but seventy times seven!

"Therefore, the Kingdom of Heaven can be compared to a king who decided to bring his accounts up to date with servants who had borrowed money from him. In the process, one of his debtors was brought in who owed him millions of dollars. He couldn't pay, so his master ordered that he be sold—along with his wife, his children, and everything he owned—to pay the debt.

"But the man fell down before his master and begged him, 'Please, be patient with me, and I will pay it all.' Then his master was filled with pity for him, and he released him and forgave his debt.

"But when the man left the king, he went to a fellow servant who owed him a few thousand dollars. He grabbed him by the throat and demanded instant payment.

"His fellow servant fell down before him and begged for a little more time. 'Be patient with me, and I will pay it,' he pleaded. But his creditor wouldn't wait. He had the man arrested and put in prison until the debt could be paid in full.

"When some of the other servants saw this, they were very upset. They went to the king and told him everything that had happened. Then the king called in the man he had forgiven and said, 'You evil servant! I forgave you that tremendous debt because you pleaded with me. Shouldn't you have mercy on your fellow servant, just as I had mercy on you?' Then the angry king sent the man to prison to be tortured until he had paid his entire debt.

"That's what my heavenly Father will do to you if you refuse to forgive your brothers and sisters from your heart." (NLT)

There are certain things that we are meant to lose track of. Accounting principles will keep us out of trouble financially but they do not govern human life. For example, in the first chapter of Numbers King David was told to *"count"* the people of Israel – to take a census. There was another occasion, recorded in 2Samuel 24, when he took a census that proved to be a grievous sin and took a heavy toll in lives. Counting is going on in our brain all the time, but for some people with emotional or mental irregularities, conscious, controlled counting is a life and death issue vital to their emotional equilibrium. A well-known example is portrayed in the TV show, Monk.

In biblical philosophy, this fixation on countable things, important but superficial things, is actually a clear sign of mental, moral or even spiritual instability. Actions result from motivations. Motivations issue from what holds highest value. If someone's financial gain is of highest value, it is obvious to anyone who cares to notice the actions of that person. If intimate relationship with Jesus is the most valuable thing to someone, attitude and actions broadcast that message.

By his question, what would you say is most important to Peter? We might immediately say that it was approval from God, righteousness. That ambition is truly admirable. However, the method by which we choose to gain what is most important to us, is just as important. We've heard it said that we must do God's work in God's way. In fact, the entire panorama of Scripture points to knowing Him *including* His ways as the central issue.

The rules (basis for any accounting) are replaced steadily by our better knowing Him and His intent behind His giving the rulings and the accountings. The replacement happens in daily interaction with Jesus the Messiah. So Peter had gotten the proper priority through the Law, but was confused about the means by which it was to be acquired.

Righteousness, if that is our goal, is acquired in one way. That way completely forgets about counting, and simply loves God and allows Him to do what He does in us without it having to "add up" or make sense to us. So, as this relates to FORGIVENESS, we lose track. We can't count up the times that forgiveness is asked for and given with a quota or limit in mind. We just FORGIVE. Why? Because that is God's WAY.

Then Jesus appears to throw in a real whiplash as He tells a story about a king, two debtors and forgiveness. His story illustrates what happens when we forget to forget. It seems He has much more important pursuits for us to be engaged in than spending our time counting and keeping track. If we begin to count and place quotas and limits on our application of forgiveness, then all accounts forgiven us ARE REVERSED.

I haven't heard much preaching on this one. I wonder why. Could it be we are just as confused as Peter was? Could it be that we need the same Helper that Peter needed to clear up for us what is required? It obviously was cleared up for Peter on the day of Pentecost. Maybe we need a big bunch of that. Recently, that waiting and being still before the Lord has become very important.

Chapter Twenty Eight

PASSING THE TEST(ers)
Matthew 19:1-9

*W*hen Jesus had finished saying these things, he left Galilee and went down to the region of Judea east of the Jordan River. Large crowds followed him there, and he healed their sick.

Some Pharisees came and tried to trap him with this question: "Should a man be allowed to divorce his wife for just any reason?" "Haven't you read the Scriptures?" Jesus replied. "They record that from the beginning God made them male and female." And he said, "This explains why a man leaves his father and mother and is joined to his wife, and the two are united into one. Since they are no longer two but one, let no one split apart what God has joined together." "Then why did Moses say in the law that a man could give his wife a written notice of divorce and send her away?" they asked. Jesus replied, "Moses permitted divorce only as a concession to your hard hearts, but it was not what God had originally intended. And I tell you this, whoever divorces his wife and marries someone else commits adultery—unless his wife has been unfaithful." (NLT)

The Pharisees were always brewing tests for Jesus. They don't seem to be too bright though. They keep doing it even though He shreds them every time. If it weren't so pitiful, it would be great comedy!

Consider another even more tragically comedic perspective on this phenomena by pondering two questions:

1) Who is behind the tests? (Hint: see Matthew 4:1-11) *"Then Jesus was led by the [Holy] Spirit into the wilderness to be tempted by the devil..."*

2) What if the tests were actually designed, scripted? Be careful. This is not contradictory to James' absolutely true declaration that no one is tempted *by God*. Notice that it was the Holy Spirit that "*led Jesus*

*into the wilderness to be tempted **by the devil**.*" Also, notice the model prayer that Jesus taught us, "*...and lead us not into temptation...*"

Too strange a thought? What if all tests, I mean, *all* tests, along with everything else that was designed before the foundations of the world, were designed, scripted and scheduled by God? For what purpose? Why would God do such a thing? What if all tests were designed for the purpose of exposing the stark contrast between the devil's spirit of insanity and the brilliant Spirit of Power, Love and Sanity, in the pure Light of Jesus?

I don't mean to trivialize Lucifer and the rest of his duped lackeys. On the other hand, it is just possible that humans' existence in this physical, tangible, time/space world is, at least in part, to show the whole world just how deranged this *"Star of the Morning"* is in his rejection of God's grace. And if that is possible, then it would be safe to say that Lucifer's deepest suffering is inflicted when a human being resolutely turns from self-obsessed foolishness to give themselves – heart, mind, body and spirit – to Jesus.

The devil's tests at the beginning of Jesus' public ministry were focused on his best illusion. It is called "the three pillars of a human being's felt needs." They are alleged to be the appetites of the body, of the eyes and of the ego.

Now, in this scene, the religious elite present a test that is focused on the laws of human conduct. These are the laws that Jesus condensed into two for us: 1. *Love God,* 2. *Love each other.* By this, Jesus establishes the foundation and priority of all relationship. Relationship is the natural result of the Nature of God living and working in a redeemed and surrendered human being. It is the distinction between Individuality and Personality, the state of one – isolated; the other – integrated. There had been a compromise in the law relating to marriage. Moses, the secondary lawgiver, had relaxed the statement of purpose from God, the primary Lawgiver. If this test was indeed scripted by God, the purpose was surely to restore the original concept. In fact, back in Matthew 5, Jesus points out several of these issues in such terms as, *"You've heard it said..., but I tell you..."* The one all-encompassing purpose for His coming was to restore all things to their original definitions and relational function, especially in human beings.

In this passage it is clear that what had been revered as an authorized revision (the especially sacred ones are those that facilitate our convenience) could no longer be tolerated. This deplorable cultural practice had been going on since the time of Moses! Why? *"Because of the hardness of their hearts."* What exactly does that mean? Plainly, it means that they refused to let love rule their hearts and actions. They deified their own base desire and relative convenience.

The purpose for marriage, one man + one woman, is so rudimentary that we miss it. It is the "lab" God designed for a male and female to learn, practice and model the original design, which by the Fall was corrupted, leaving them inherently disabled in the relational functions of love (male) and respect (female). The corrupted DNA was accomplished by replacing those original functions with a void sequence – Isolated Personal Sovereignty, a basic element of Satan worship. Therefore, marriage is the world's stage on which Man's transformation from the domination of a satanic disposition, to God's gracious gathering disposition, can be observed and infect the world with the courage to be victorious in the supreme human test.

It is not necessary to go into the integral part the Holy Spirit has to play in that process. The essence and fruit of God's Spirit, which reconstitutes us, *IS* love *[=joy, peace, long-suffering, kindness, goodness, faithfulness, gentleness and self-control], in contrast to the fruit of Satan's spirit* [=sexual immorality, impurity, lustful pleasures, idolatry, sorcery, hostility, quarreling, jealousy, outbursts of anger, selfish ambition, dissension, division, envy, drunkenness, wild parties, etc. (Galatians 5)].

The TEST designed for that? <u>MARRIAGE</u> (Matt 19:4-5 AMPC). He replied, *"Have you never read that He who made them from the beginning made them male and female?"* And said, *"For this reason a man shall leave his father and mother and shall be united firmly (joined inseparably) to his wife, and the two shall become one flesh"* (see Gen 2:24 AMP).

Clearly, in Jesus' mind divorce is not rational (verse 9). It is totally out of context unless that context has been destroyed by moral rebellion. The one who initiates the divorce or the fornication, destroys that context and fails the test and creates a crater that the whole family falls into, along with their circle of friends and acquaintances.

Marriage is the triathlon of the relational arena in which the dominion of the nature of God can be tangibly tested. Are we passing? God's tests are cluster bombs to display to the world the contrast between the Truth and the Lie and those who follow each.

Chapter Twenty Nine

ALTERNATIVE?
Matthew 19:11-12

*B**ut He said to them, "All cannot accept this saying, but only those to whom it has been given: For there are eunuchs who were born thus from their mother's womb, and there are eunuchs who were made eunuchs by men, and there are eunuchs who have made themselves eunuchs for the kingdom of heaven's sake. He who is able to accept it, let him accept it."* (NKJV)

I'm afraid we don't actually hear what Jesus says sometimes merely because we don't understand or don't feel comfortable with the subject matter. *Eunuch*, in any dictionary means: *a person who has been castrated, therefore has no reproductive capacity or activity.* Another use of the word in the Old Testament was in reference to a court official. That court official was especially focused on his job and therefore especially trustworthy, because he had no family or sexual distractions. That doesn't change the source definition. It only points to a particular useful capacity of a eunuch [see https://en.wikipedia.org/wiki/Eunuch].

A modern parallel is the discovery that autistic people have become valuable workers because they are wired to intensely focus on the one thing they are working on. Now that we've established that, we can go on to explore what Jesus is saying.

Read again the verses we focused on last time. Jesus has bluntly disclosed Heaven's view of marriage in contrast to the irrational concept of divorce. Then, because the guys go, "Well then, what's the use?", He discloses another of Heaven's insights. In essence, there is an alternative – the official "alternative lifestyle."

The alternative to marriage (one man with one woman for life) is NO, NONE, ZERO sexual activity. If God's Book is our standard for life, we must get this straight. [Pun intended] Any sex outside God's model of marriage is called a whole lot of things in Heaven but not one of them is "alternative lifestyle!" It is not life at all. It is more like invasion of the walking dead. Unless we can accept as life-or-death truth that our physical appetites are *not* equal to, much less higher than God's design for human life, we will not be able to even read or believe what He has written in His Book without altering it to suit our taste. That is why it is so hard to draw moral lines in a humanistic, totally secular-psychology-driven social environment. Human nature is so obsessively worshiped that it becomes the standard, therefore actual rules or absolutes cannot be taken seriously. That is the real-life drama of people who are referred to as "perishing," the walking dead. But the moment we are ready to accept that God, the Creator of the whole world, has offered intimate fellowship with Himself as the antidote for the self-destruction that the broken human nature produces, the veil is lifted from our eyes. There are many reasons for curbing our appetites, but the only one we need at that point is that God said to. He made humans for perpetually-refreshed, gloriously-fulfilling fellowship. That is the brand name – LIFE.

Let me just expand on one of psychologists' observations regarding pedophilia, which asserts: "It is predatory. That makes it bad." "Bad", of course, being a relative term, which means judged by whatever my current opinion dictates. Pedophiles are lobbying to get on the list of deviants looking to get government recognition and tax relief for their clubs where they shop for and devour the bodies of children. They actually want the income from their clubs' operations to be tax-free. First, there's same-sex marriage, then same-sex toilets, then gender-choice for kindergarteners, and coming soon to your neighborhood perhaps, mixed human-to-animal marriages. Perpetrators of the most heinous crimes of perversion against human beings are actually lobbying for government tax relief. Believe me, government recognition is a very temporary covering in light of what is in store for them long-long-term. Remember the millstone?

The bottom-line is this: All sex outside God's design for marriage is predatory. That includes marriages that are strictly appetite driven. Those marriages are living cannibalism; there is a predator and a prey. There is a perpetrator and a victim...a CRIME, with all the aftermath of a crime, including personal trauma and damage or death to the soul. In Heaven, the delusion is obvious. In the heart of a human born-again by the Spirit of God, the delusion is obvious. To put it lightly, it calls wrong, right and right, wrong. Surely you have noticed that it is only those who have been early prey who become the predators and promoters of its social acceptance. Of course, they want it to be accepted, normal, and even pretty because it is between "consenting adults." That alone verifies beyond debate that the delusion is diabolical. They are the ones who are bruised and bleeding, psychologically damaged, unable to think rationally or objectively about anything, because the predator's claws are still embedded and sinking deeper and deeper into their souls, forcing them to become their own victims.

The fact is, God has provided the cure and it is not just a rule to follow. He has given Himself. He offers Himself, the cure, to anyone who even glimpses the desperate results of the path they walk. Even our idea of goodness falls far short of what is demanded by our own heart when we see God, our Father, and hear His voice calling our name. We hear the affection and steady, unstoppable love of a Father longing for His child just to acknowledge Him and begin to enjoy being His son or daughter with real Family resemblance. That's the only Doorway to reality, to freedom.

Having given Himself, God is full of rejoicing, not weeping. All Heaven has joined in with the Father's celebration at the return of His once-lost sons and daughters. It is suggested that CS Lewis said, "He's pretending we are just like His Son Jesus, until we pass this veil of time and space and it becomes a reality."

It is profoundly futile, in view of eternity,
to even spend one breath of my life in service to,
or in defense of, my ways.
Nothing will fully satisfy
but to see my Father face to face.
Oh, what a day that will be!
Oh, what a day!

Chapter Thirty

PERSPECTIVE
Matthew 19:13-15

*O*ne day some parents brought their children to Jesus so he could lay his hands on them and pray for them. But the disciples scolded the parents for bothering him. But Jesus said, "Let the children come to me. Don't stop them! For the Kingdom of Heaven belongs to those who are like these children." And he placed his hands on their heads and blessed them before he left. (NLT)

Perspective is crucial equipment for human beings and has some provocative properties. Perspective has to do with our varying relationship to objects ranging from close to far away. Perspective empowers us to distinguish between the ones in the foreground and those in the distance. Human beings are normally equipped with two eyes for precisely this purpose. Having two eyes a little distance apart sends pictures from two different points making the resulting composite picture three-dimensional. And, may I add, quite a bit safer to navigate.

A science lesson at this point may seem a little odd, but I've often found great insight as I study the rudimentary facts of how God designed things and I would like for you to taste the wonder of that, too. It is His own Spirit that He has installed in us, that can give us a direct line to understanding His reality. That intimate connection to Him provides eyes to see and understand the messages He has embedded in every single thing He made in our physical reality. Every distinct emanation of His genius is a hint, a shadow of something real, something eternal. In light of that, the words of Romans 8:22-23 are very compelling, *"We know that until now, the whole creation has been groaning as with the pains of childbirth; and not only it, but we ourselves, who have the firstfruits of the Spirit, groan inwardly as we continue waiting eagerly to be made sons – that is, to have our whole bodies redeemed and set free"* [CJB].

We must also know that perspective is the first thing that is lost when a human being submits to self-absorption or creedal dogma. And we are crippled if our cognitive instincts such as perspective, discernment, wisdom or common sense are lost or become atrophied. Try this experiment: Put a patch on one eye for even just an hour and discover the danger in moving from place to place with only one point of view.

The basic point to make first here is that to have perspective we must have more than one point of view. One person's point of view never equals perspective and therefore is insufficient for any authentic determination. Therefore, the universal Law of God's creation in respect to judgment is that it must never be decided based on the word of only one eye witness.

Secondly, the added point of view must be actual as opposed to assumed, and factual not fabricated. It is not good enough to guess what someone else is thinking, and add that to go along with our opinion. That seems pretty trivial until we start to remember how easy it is to make a quick conclusion based on a plausible report and how many times we have acted on presumption.

Lastly, that added point of view should ideally belong to someone who has learned this lesson of perspective, and habitually requires an additional point of view from someone more insightful than themselves. This is the prescription for a growing maturity and fruitfulness. There is only one absolutely guaranteed point of view on any subject – God's. And Jesus said, "Father, I have done all You sent Me to do." "I only say what I hear my Father say. I only do what I see Him do." "If you really knew the Father, you would have recognized Me" (John 5:19; 12:49; 14:7; 17:4). So, His is the ideal point of view to always add, no matter how many others have been considered. "Here's what I think, but what does Jesus think?" That needs to be the habitual conversation with myself, always turning then to conversation with Him before I say it or put it in writing. If not, my reactions can be as inappropriate as the disciples' before their immersion into the Holy Spirit.

"...the disciples rebuked them" (parents and children). They what? Jesus said, "*Let the children come to Me!*" If we think Jesus was always soft spoken and sympathetic toward presumptive ignorance, we need to read His Book, the whole Book, until we get to know Him. The Holy Spirit has been given to us to make available the guaranteed perspective from Jesus' point of view. No one has said it more direct than in Paul's letter to the Church in Corinth:

"But, as the Tanakh says, 'No eye has seen, no ear has heard and no one's heart has imagined all the things that God has prepared for those who love him.' It is to us, however, that God has revealed these things. How? Through the Spirit. For the Spirit probes all things, even the profoundest depths of God. For who knows the inner workings of a person except the person's own spirit inside him? So too, no one knows the inner workings of God except God's Spirit. Now we have not received the spirit of the world but the Spirit of God, so that we might understand the things God has so freely given us. These are the things we are talking about when we avoid the manner of speaking that human wisdom would dictate and instead use a manner of speaking taught by the Spirit, by which we explain things of the Spirit to people who have the Spirit. Now the natural man does not receive the things from the Spirit of God — to him they are nonsense! Moreover, he is unable to grasp them, because they are evaluated through the Spirit. But the person who has the Spirit can evaluate everything, while no one is in a position to evaluate him. For who has known the mind of Adonai? Who will counsel him? But we have the mind of the Messiah" (1Corinthians 2:9-16 CJB).

Surely we, as His followers, agree that we need to see everything through Jesus' eyes. So why do we continue to build structure and policy into our lives and organizations, then continue to develop them and operate by them, without consulting Him? The structure and policy seem to be needed and called for, but often that's verifiably because they afford us some illusion of convenience, increased efficiency or even elevated importance.

In regard to children, we [the church culture] either farm them out so they won't interrupt; or we [parents] deify them by centering everything around what they want or need, thus avoiding the hard work of disciplining them. They shouldn't be kept from coming to us and being with us, but just as important, their every feeling is not to be catered to when they are with us. They are to be blessed and taught and touched by us as we go about our routines of life in the home and community, but especially in worship and Body life. Perhaps our hardest relational work is to disciple our own children. Discipline is crucial, but is only one part of bringing them up in the admonition of the Lord [the Lord's personal training]. Actually, no... it's the second hardest. The hardest work is having to learn basic discipline after reaching adulthood! So, the kindest most responsible thing to do for our children is to take the time and make the effort while their circuits are still being connected, to lead them into a knowing relationship with God by the daily washing of His Word and intimate conversation with Him. If we wait till after they are six years old, we will smart for it and so will they. I would venture to conclude that, in Heaven, that particular application of hesitancy is found over in the file drawer labeled, RETARDED. All through God's Book, that job is firmly in the responsibility of parents. Yes, there a whole world of participation, but that participation better be verified as harmonious and supporting Jesus personal training program. Case in point: In the '50s the U.S. government decided to take that burden of responsibility off the shoulders of the increasingly busy young families engaged in "making a good living" so they could buy new stuff and be respectable. We are all experiencing the continued and mounting layers of consequences.

PERSPECTIVE: THE DIMENSIONS OF REAL LIFE

We have perspective because we have Jesus and His absolutely trustworthy point of view, the Holy Spirit. We acknowledge our need for Him, ask Him for His perspective and walk by it. *His* is the added point of view that gives us sure footing and a fruitful path. Fruitful according to God's definition in terms of "***now and forever.***" (see Romans 8:6-8 AMP)

For God did not give us a spirit of timidity or cowardice *or* fear, but [He has given us a spirit] of *power and of love and of sound judgment and* personal discipline [abilities that result in a calm, well-balanced mind and self-*control]* (2Timothy 1:7 AMP).

Chapter Thirty One

LIKE CHILDREN
Matthew 19:14

*B*ut Jesus said, "Let the children come to me. Don't stop them! For the Kingdom of Heaven belongs to those who are like these children." (NLT)

Most of the exposition I have heard about what Jesus is saying, focuses on childlikeness, the requirement for entering the Kingdom of Heaven (see Mark 10 & Luke 18). It is certainly Truth to point to children with no pretense; who are spontaneous, unaffected, giggling or gushing tears and say, "That's what the Kingdom is like." On the other hand, there is one action commanded of all who would be a resident in God's Household – "*Come to me.*" The sheer volume of reference to this foundational command makes it very possible that Jesus is talking about how inappropriate it is for the disciples to bar anyone and especially the children from coming to Him.

Taking in account the panorama of Scripture, this is the centerpiece of our participation in God's gift of salvation. We can add nothing to the cross to enhance its power to save. The only power we humans have is the power of choice, to choose to turn and come toward Jesus, **or not**. We can break that action down into two obvious physical images, turning and coming, primarily because many have turned toward Him but have not come to Him, which affects more than the individual. That half-action is precisely what produces the scene we are looking at in this verse. Here are "disciples" who have turned toward Jesus, but do not yet *come to Him*, only because they haven't a clue what He is like or what He is up to. They are clearly still depending on their own lone point of view as the basis for conclusions and actions.

Consider this hypothetical scene: Someone gets my attention. I turn to observe but stay at a distance. Basically, that is a counter-challenge. I am saying, "Okay, you've got my attention. Now, show me what you've got and what's in it for me." I have turned and I am aware of what's happening at a distance, but I have not moved toward that someone. I HAVE NOT COME.

The nature of that posture produces a wall that discourages those around me from coming as well, a much more serious matter than to exclude childish behavior because it might interrupt or distract someone or, heaven forbid, draw attention to itself. That exclusion is priggish enough, but the gravity is in the more fundamental mistake – attempting to look like a participant when the families are segregated physically and spiritually. Interpreting a "potential of distraction" as a dreaded danger in the gathering of a congregation and then installing corporate policies to establish age-sensitive segmentation of the Body, blocks discovery of what God wants to say to us and what we would be doing if we, as a family, heard what He said and obeyed together. In light of culture's almost 60 years of systematic dismantling the family, that is very possibly a grave mistake. We misinterpret the heart of Jesus when we exclude parts of the family from our corporal time of worship in the Word and response to Jesus as the family of God, gathered around the Head of the family.

The essence of Jesus' invitation to "come" means to *be joined*. Not just become one of the pack, like an animal, but become ONE with Him. The Holy Spirit will have to continue to draw us toward this joining in Jesus because as long as we are in these bodies, with these minds, we will be vacillating and battling with the obstinacy of our programed instincts and appetites. But His mercy is new every morning – for good reason! We need that open door and welcoming invitation every time we are drawn away by our own lusts, obstinacy or even willful ignorance.

The tension this revelation seems to pose, between being adults and being children, is irrational to our natural minds. How can I be a child, being already past that? Sounds like Nicodemus' response to *"You must be born again"* (John 3:4). That is the key that unlocks, if we want it to. The *"Kingdom of Heaven"* has to be illustrated to us by certain parallels in our reality, the time and space world, which is only the shadow of the reality of Heaven (see Colossians 2, Hebrews 8 & 10). Jesus even refers to that in the rest of His explanation to Nicodemus in John 3:5-21.

We have to stop trying to define God's world and where He wants us to come, by our own insight and knowledge. Even our most true expression of His revelation to us is but a shadow of what the Holy Spirit will progressively reveal, and especially in the case of what it means – *"to come."*

Yes, what it is to "come to Him" will be a mystery up to that point of our abandoning the silliness of defining it based only in our own experience or knowledge. But the one who will set aside previous, though true, understanding and expectation, and simply come to Jesus; is a fully converted organism fit to be a building block in the Body of Christ (see Matt 16:18 & Eph 2).

Be the Body. Come to Him. Right where He put us. Not to some work that we can define in our own mind. He is calling us past all the shadows, to Himself – right now, right here where He has put us. We need not move geographically to come to Him, He is right here, even in our heart. That is the initial part of the call of the Spirit, to come to Jesus. Even if He happens to take us all over the world, surrender starts right where we are and, no, it is of no concern of ours where He wants to go or what He wants to do in our skin, unless and until He deems that we have, what they call in the Military, "the need to know." We are One in Him, one of His distributed and synchronized set of boots on the ground in this world. Believe His promise to lead a step at a time. Our job is to enjoy Him and follow. By that, we know Him better with every step we take in His footprints. HALLELUYAH! THANK YOU, JESUS!

Chapter Thirty Two

RELIGIOUS AIRS
Matthew 19:16-30

*S*omeone came to Jesus with this question: "Teacher, what good things must I do to have eternal life?" "Why ask me about what is good?" Jesus replied. "Only God is good. But to answer your question, you can receive eternal life if you keep the commandments."

"Which ones?" the man asked. And Jesus replied: "Do not murder. Do not commit adultery. Do not steal. Do not testify falsely. Honor your father and mother. Love your neighbor as yourself." "I've obeyed all these commandments," the young man replied. "What else must I do?" Jesus told him, "If you want to be perfect, go and sell all you have and give the money to the poor, and you will have treasure in heaven. Then come, follow me." But when the young man heard this, he went sadly away because he had many possessions.

Then Jesus said to his disciples, "I tell you the truth, it is very hard for a rich person to get into the Kingdom of Heaven. I say it again--it is easier for a camel to go through the eye of a needle than for a rich person to enter the Kingdom of God!"

The disciples were astounded. "Then who in the world can be saved?" they asked. Jesus looked at them intently and said, "Humanly speaking, it is impossible. But with God everything is possible."

Then Peter said to him, "We've given up everything to follow you. What will we get out of it?"

And Jesus replied, "I assure you that when I, the Son of Man, sit upon my glorious throne in the Kingdom, you who have been my followers will also sit on twelve thrones, judging the twelve tribes of Israel. And everyone who has given up houses or brothers or sisters or father or mother or children or property, for my sake, will receive a hundred times as much in return and will have eternal life. But many who seem to be important now will be the least important then, and those who are considered least here will be the greatest then." (NLT 1996)

There are many important revelations of the nature of God in this scene. I especially have been interested by the concise manner in which Jesus answered the man's questions and then did not pursue or try to persuade, though He loved him [conveyed in Mark & Luke]. But one angle in particular hasn't been dealt with as much as others.

Jesus, to all ears, especially Matthew's, is exposing the pretentious airs that religious perceptions can produce. *"What good thing must I do?... I've done that, what else?"* Jesus' final answer made that man turn and *go away sad.* Yes, *"...sad..., because He was wealthy,"* are the emotional trigger words that strikes people. But, the most spiritually demolishing camera angle on this dialog is that this man opens the door to Jesus when the Spirit knocked, but his response to Jesus' answer is to *close* the door and go back into his house to be with his stuff. That is the live-action Jesus was watching. The "sadness" was only remorse for not being able to enter with the ticket he thought he had bought – all the wealth he had acquired and all the "right" stuff he had done. The same door he had opened, he has shut in Jesus' face and turned away in a pout and Jesus did not pursue the man or attempt to explain.

That entire scene exposes what was in the young man's heart from the moment he decided to approach Jesus, and throughout the whole interaction which, of course, Jesus knew because *"He knows what is in man's heart"* (John2:23-25). That insight leads to understanding what Jesus *didn't* do, as well as what He did do. He illustrated the strong natural odds against a rich man entering the Kingdom of Heaven [turning over his heart, mind and body to be annexed as territory exclusively ruled by the King of Heaven, earth and all Creation].

Peter, following his religious reflexes says, *"We've given up everything... what will we get?"* Jesus answers, *"You'll get all that and much more in return, but your perception of personal importance is upside down!"*

Our world's market-oriented economy today is based on how important a product makes us feel, rather than the actual value the product adds to our life and work. Actual value has taken a back seat to perceived effect on our quest for self-realization and personal significance.

The enemy of God and Christian faith is not Islam or any other religion developed by man in history. All man-made Garden-born, deceptive religions reflect their real mother – the original alternative life-style – Independent Personal Sovereignty. If we want followers, we only have to promise personal independence and controlling influence over circumstances and other people. If we want to sell a product, we only have to suggest self-promotion or self-improvement.

There are only two religions in the world: devotion to our Creator, King and Savior; and the delusion suggested by His enemy who poses as an angel of light. Every marketed "enlightenment" outside the Word-of-God-made-flesh (Jesus), is darkness and deadly sucker-bait. "Satan" is the biblical name for that global delusion, which is a system pieced together from parts of truth, mixed with self-worship – the "gospel" always preached by the phony money-driven "church,inc".

So, if we want to warm our hands, satisfy our "felt-needs," be enlightened by the fires of market-oriented, mall-religion (name it whatever you like), the warmth we receive from it will soon be replaced with the icy words of Jesus when we stand before Him. If we respond to His gracious nudges to get our attention, all our self-generated comforts will disappear like the Emperor's new clothes, in the light of His love and eternal reality.

It's simple. Too simple really, for us to take any credit. We don't need to try to be "better," but be reconciled to God. That is possible only by identification with the one God sent, His only begotten Son [His one and only personally inseminated Son], Yeshua, the Messiah of God. He has redeemed us! It is imperative that we get reconciled to that! There is nothing in our nature from which to draw that kind of purity. Look to the Cross. There's the proof. He did for us, in full, what we could not do for ourselves and He did it while we were still pushing away from Him and slamming the door in His face.

Now, the question is: Will we have the courage to live out that redemption? As He brings aspects of our nature into His light, will we give way for His Nature to overrule, to consume all that is not of Him in the fire of His holiness? He exposes those squatters in His time, because He means to exchange each of them for the uncorrupted, full original version of what they are impersonating and perverting. And He wants our committed participation in the uninstall, new install and daily maintenance. "Yes, Please!" is the only sane answer!

We can go for it! All the hosts of Heaven are cheering us on!

NOTE: Matthew's journal records a little different angle on Jesus' conversation with this man, best known as "the rich young ruler," than that of Mark's or Dr. Luke's, with which we are probably more familiar only because of the volume of references in messages heard. Those two journals record that the man referred to Jesus as "*Good teacher*," to which Jesus came back with, "*Why do you call me good? There's none good but God!*" They also reveal the insider scoop that "*Jesus felt love for him* *and said, 'One thing you lack,'* followed by His prescription. Whether the conversation takes a different tack for different ears or the familiar title given to the man is a correct description of him or not, the final punch line for all disciples is the same… entry to the Kingdom – impossible, except with God. *"All things are possible with God."*

Chapter Thirty Three

TRUST YOUR OWN PERCEPTION?
Matthew 20:1-19

"*For the Kingdom of Heaven is like the owner of an estate who went out early one morning to hire workers for his vineyard. He agreed to pay the normal daily wage and sent them out to work.*

At nine o'clock in the morning he was passing through the marketplace and saw some people standing around doing nothing. So he hired them, telling them he would pay them whatever was right at the end of the day.

At noon and again around three o'clock he did the same thing. At five o'clock that evening he was in town again and saw some more people standing around. He asked them, 'Why haven't you been working today?' They replied, 'Because no one hired us.' The owner of the estate told them, 'Then go on out and join the others in my vineyard.'

That evening he told the foreman to call the workers in and pay them, beginning with the last workers first. When those hired at five o'clock were paid, each received a full day's wage. When those hired earlier came to get their pay, they assumed they would receive more. But they, too, were paid a day's wage. When they received their pay, they protested, 'Those people worked only one hour, and yet you've paid them just as much as you paid us who worked all day in the scorching heat.'

He answered one of them, 'Friend, I haven't been unfair! Didn't you agree to work all day for the usual wage? Take it and go. I wanted to pay this last worker the same as you. Is it against the law for me to do what I want with my money? Should you be angry because I am kind?' And so it is, that many who are first now will be last then; and those who are last now will be first then."

As Jesus was on the way to Jerusalem, he took the twelve disciples aside privately and told them what was going to happen to him. "When we get to Jerusalem," He said, "the Son of Man will be betrayed to the leading priests and the teachers of religious law. They will sentence him to die. Then they will hand him over to the Romans to be mocked, whipped, and crucified. But on the third day he will be raised from the dead." (NLT 1996)

Take an overview approach to these words, which will further illustrate, in parable as well as live-action, the point Jesus makes at the end of Chapter 19 – Things are not really how they seem to us. In fact, most of our natural way of evaluating situations and people is foreign to the way God made them, sometimes even completely opposite. He is specifically talking about the way we put people into categories or ranks of importance.

His first illustration is a parable, a story about an estate owner who hires people throughout the day for the work that he needs done. He points to the natural calculations based on the duration of the job. Then He contrasts the natural view with the perspective and prerogative of the owner. He can do what he wants with his money and he decides to pay everyone a full day's wage, though some worked all day and others barely worked at all.

The common view of employee/management situations responds by concluding that the owner was unfair. But the parable is not meant to establish a new policy for businesses and factories, it is meant to reveal something pivotal about the nature of God. If we are inclined to look at things through our natural, "common sense" eyes, we immediately agree with the worker who is not happy and we promptly join his class-action suit against the owner – but for what? He received a full day's wage, which he agreed to. If he hadn't been privy to what the owner paid the others, he would have gone home very pleased and satisfied that he had put in a full day's work and got a full day's wage. But he watches as the openly intentional owner first calls the ones who had just gotten there and pays them what he expected to get paid for the full day. He begins to have a flush of excitement because he would naturally get much more. That excitement turns to disappointment when he receives the same amount.

Jesus is saying two very simple things almost too simple for our adult constitutions to receive. First: God can do what He wants. He is God, not subject to common sense or religious sensitivities. He doesn't take into consideration our expectations and conclusions, no matter how right and wise they may seem to us. Second: The same salvation is offered to every one who calls on the name of the LORD. Saved is saved is saved. Remember what Jesus said when the disciples came back from their missionary trip rejoicing because the demons obeyed them? "Don't rejoice in that. Rejoice because you are a registered resident of heaven" (Luke 10:20).

Neither personal effort nor ability is a factor in the equation. That's a great thing for those of us who are not Paul the apostle or Billy Graham or have not even been a Christian for very long. God offered salvation; we took it; we're saved – HALLELUYAH! The *only* thing we did was take it. The rest is His doing too. He can do what He wants. Our part is letting Him. His plan can be that we're a smiling, happy, blessed, influential Christian or a persecuted, broken, impoverished, despised Christian. The point is, HEY we're saved! The external wrapping is just the context in which He illustrates the irrefutable, earth-shattering proof that His salvation is for everyone. There is no more powerful witness of the truth of God's existence than a saved human being.

Then as a personal revelation of this very concept, the LORD of lords, King of kings, Name above all names, draws the disciples aside and tells them in effect, "I, God incarnate, the highest of all - will become the lowest. I am going to be despised, broken, impoverished and killed" (vs 18-19).

"The first will be last and the last will be first." This reveals a whole new meaning to *"I am the first AND the last."*

The important thing to get here is that we don't see things like God sees them. The installation of that one little warning light flashing across the bottom of the screen in our little pea-brain would keep us out of a lot of trouble! There is always at least one thing that we do not know. There is most likely a multitude of things, but remembering there is at least one, *should* keep us from putting our foot in our mouth for all to see.

Chapter Thirty Four

GETTING TO THE POINT
Matthew 20:17-24

*A*s Jesus was going up to Jerusalem, he took the twelve disciples aside privately and told them what was going to happen
to him. "Listen," he said, "we're going up to Jerusalem, where
*the Son of Man will be betrayed to the leading priests and the teachers
of religious law. They will sentence him to die. Then they will hand him
over to the Romans to be mocked, flogged with a whip, and crucified.
But on the third day he will be raised from the dead."*

*Then the mother of James and John, the sons of Zebedee, came
to Jesus with her sons. She knelt respectfully to ask a favor. "What is
your request?" he asked. She replied, "In your Kingdom, please let my
two sons sit in places of honor next to you, one on your right and the
other on your left."*

*But Jesus answered by saying to them, "You don't know what you
are asking! Are you able to drink from the bitter cup of suffering I am
about to drink?"*

"Oh yes," they replied, "we are able!"

*Jesus told them, "You will indeed drink from my bitter cup.
But I have no right to say who will sit on my right or my left. My
Father has prepared those places for the ones he has chosen."
When the ten other disciples heard what James and John had asked,
they were indignant.* (NLT)

Amazing! Jesus tells the parable in the previous verses and then
they act it out! The principle in the parable is simply that God's agenda
is the only agenda, and if we are going to be in His Kingdom, fulfilling
what we are made to accomplish and be aware of it, we have to push
away from our myopic, self-interest. Oh, how our perceptions change
when the Holy Spirit opens our eyes to the real world!

But Jesus is very gracious, at least I think so, in the face of blatant self-promotion. He obviously (and invariably) sees more into their personalities than I can, yet He doesn't rebuke them at all. Instead He explains that what they want of Him had already been decided. He knew that all things had been put under His authority. He knew where He was headed and why. He also knew that they would follow soon enough.

Personally, I take deep encouragement from that scene and the gracious interaction that comes from Jesus to His disciples. I don't know a single time when I could accurately and fully predict what He has been up to with me. That has become so clear that I no longer expect to know much of anything except Him and the insight He is giving for this moment. And that, I know, is a tiny pinhole glimpse of the whole picture. I surely wouldn't know what to do with it if I saw the whole picture! But I love the echo of His love that I can hear in His voice when, instead of rebuking, He just asks a question, *"Can you...?"* He knew they had no clue what the *"cup"* was. He also knew they would share in the suffering that He was about to undergo. *"You will."*

I am certain each one of them heard the echo of those words at the moment of their graduation into His presence. They followed His instructions to the letter, *"He that saves his life... He that loses... for My sake..."* Deep loyalty to their Savior would bring them to honor their true Friend and Master by laying down their life and stepping directly into a face-to-face greeting from Him. *"Well done, good and faithful servant. Enter into the joy of your Lord."*

Nothing is worth missing that.

Chapter Thirty Five

LOOK AT JESUS!
Matthew 20:25-33

*B*ut Jesus called them together and said, "You know that the rulers in this world lord it over their people, and officials flaunt
their authority over those under them. But among you it will
be different. Whoever wants to be a leader among you must be your
servant, and whoever wants to be first among you must become your
slave. For even the Son of Man came not to be served but to serve others and to give his life as a ransom for many."

As Jesus and the disciples left the town of Jericho, a large crowd
followed behind. Two blind men were sitting beside the road. When
they heard that Jesus was coming that way, they began shouting,
"Lord, Son of David, have mercy on us!"

"Be quiet!" the crowd yelled at them.

But they only shouted louder, "Lord, Son of David, have mercy
on us!"

When Jesus heard them, he stopped and called, "What do you
want me to do for you?"

"Lord," they said, "we want to see!" Jesus felt sorry for them and
touched their eyes. Instantly they could see! Then they followed him.
(NLT)

This is very important. I repeat, **LOOK AT JESUS!**

Look at Jesus, not just someone else's interpretation of Him, no
matter how anointed and wise that person may be. Even the Word of
God itself is to lead us to know the One who is the fullness of the Word
alive in human flesh. If we stop short of knowing Him, worshiping Him,
walking in Him (though we learn about Him, sing about Him and walk
in the shadow of other men's vision of Him), we stop short of eternity by

holding to what we can reason and grasp in our own minds.

If the Bible teaches us anything, it is man's seemingly inevitable response to God's personal revelation of Himself. From the moment Adam and Eve established that response until now, we always receive the revelation of God in a cloud of misunderstanding. Then we proceed to build philosophies, social systems and organizations upon our expanded conclusions – which are based on faulty and incomplete understanding in the first place! Thus, the endless cycle:

God speaks new Life
    Man responds in Obedience
        Followed by Revelation
            That produces Pride
                Which invites Delusion
                    Which ends in Despair
                        And Death
                    God speaks new Life
                Man responds in Obedience
            Followed by Revelation
        That produces Pride
    Which invites Delusion
  Which ends in Despair
And Death

As long as we are not born of the Spirit, given entry into Jesus, we stand outside Him and our views are hopelessly skewed and sure to repeat the cycle.

I'm not talking about the world here. This is the history, ancient and current, of those God calls "My people." God has chosen to shine this spotlight on a group of people down through history to be a live illustration of the desperate straights in which the whole human race is stuck. The incredible thing to me is that He keeps perpetuating the cycle, by invading the darkness of what Man's design creates by suddenly speaking, from out of the blue. It is a good thing He's not constrained by time. If He were, He would have gotten really tired of this a very long time ago.

At certain strategic stages it seems He may have gotten tired or frustrated with the process, and just about wiped every human off the face of the earth. Clearly, that is not because He is at His wit's end and suddenly flies off the handle, but it is to show us that WE DO NOT have an infinite quantity of time. He is showing us that we are expected to receive, apply and mature to live as new creatures IN HIM – transformed and fruitful.

It is the first step of that expectation that is solely at the command of our will. We can receive His salvation or we can reject it. Every other part, even the preliminary drawing us to that point of choice, wholly issues from Him. The drawing is done by His Spirit. Even the faith it takes to believe in preparation to receive, is a gift from Him. Of course, what happens from that point through an eternity of growing usefulness and pleasure to Him, is a product of our personal, intimate communion with Him and harmony with His Spirit.

Our generation, in sync with every other generation, has decided to add another option. Previously, the clear options were, receive or reject. Now we have added another option - *designer religion*. By that I mean, Man's reasoned religion, and the systems we build to market and maintain a following for our design. Most of which is a far cry from James' definition of "*true religion*" or any other function of God's people described in His Book.

We have slipped into the stage of despair just before death, in what continues to be the inevitable cycle for man-made "religion," and therefore, the human race, as well. We've been deluded and diluted by compromise with the world's ways. We have looked away from Jesus and allowed our wandering eyes to lust after the world's delusionary brand of success, albeit in a package posing as a religious box.

From every mountain-top, every housetop, every radio and every TV set, in every interaction with other people, we are to be the heralds of God's call, "**Look at Jesus!**" Just keep looking at Him and let Him do what He does best – save and heal, reconcile and restore, touch and transform. Don't try to be Jesus. Don't try to be the Holy Spirit. We invite delusion when that self-effort begins to follow the natural enthusiasm of our own heart. Jesus is real and alive. He is fully able to complete what He has begun. The Holy Spirit doesn't need as much help from us as we think. The more we "help," the more we get in the way and distract from His own supernatural work in the hearts of men and women, boys and girls.

Just keep looking at Jesus. Know Him in the intimacy He wants with us, not what we conjure up when we feel it and then fades when we don't. He's right there. Love and desire Him enough to talk to Him. Ask Him to make Himself real and fill every dark corner of our heart and imagination with the light and refreshing oil of His Spirit; His Spirit of love and purpose and hope, His all-powerful disposition of patience and kindness, sanity and courage.

It is good to learn what God is saying through His Word, His Prophets and Apostles. But it is not given to us just to learn the words and expect others to interpret them as we do. We must go on to where God has called us and be the genuine worshipers He is looking for *now*. Filled with His Spirit *now*. Loving like He loves and walking in the joy of our salvation, which is: TO BE WITH HIM, in spite of every trial or attempted delusion; in the face of every distraction and surprise twist in the road.

Those trials, distractions and detours are not the *enemy* but the *rooting* of our faith and the qualifiers for our place with Him in eternity. Our enemy is not the demons or infidels out there. The enemy, the infidel, is our own heart, a heart that will take the easy way or the popular way or the devious way of covering our guilt with angry tirades. Thus, evading the Doorway to eternity with Him - to be God's child, His man, His woman.

Jesus is the Key! *Look at Him.* Don't focus on the wrath of God, that was illustrated simply to clarify our desperate situation. In the face of hope in the Law of Moses or the demands of Muhammad or the escapism of Buda or the forces of nature, Jesus is the Key that opens God's love and redemption to His beloved creation. We have lived too long, held in the grip of laws and demands.

The Key has been there in plain sight all along. Take the Key. Pick it up. Yes, it is dirty and blood spattered. That is because He is one of us, and that dirt and blood is the inevitable effect of the law of sin and death on flesh and blood. Pick it up and put it in the lock. Allow Him to fill with the love that conquers all the darkness, simply because it heals and opens our infidel heart.

Tho' He slay me, yet will I serve Him.
For the joy set before Him?
We are that joy.
Look at Jesus.
Get past the cloud of Man's devices
and see Him, face to face.
That is the only reality we need.
He is the only reality.
He that keeps seeking will find.
To him who persists in knocking
the door will be opened.
Look at Jesus and ask, seek and knock, till...

Chapter Thirty Six

TRIUMPHAL ENTRY?
Matthew 21:1-11

*A*s Jesus and the disciples approached Jerusalem, they came to the town of Bethphage on the Mount of Olives. Jesus sent two of them on ahead. "Go into the village over there," he said. "As soon as you enter it, you will see a donkey tied there, with its colt beside it. Untie them and bring them to me. If anyone asks what you are doing, just say, 'The Lord needs them,' and he will immediately let you take them."

This took place to fulfill the prophecy that said, "Tell the people of Israel, 'Look, your King is coming to you. He is humble, riding on a donkey—riding on a donkey's colt.'"

The two disciples did as Jesus commanded. They brought the donkey and the colt to him and threw their garments over the colt, and he sat on it.

Most of the crowd spread their garments on the road ahead of him, and others cut branches from the trees and spread them on the road. Jesus was in the center of the procession, and the people all around him were shouting, "Praise God for the Son of David! Blessings on the one who comes in the name of the Lord! Praise God in highest heaven!"

The entire city of Jerusalem was in an uproar as he entered. "Who is this?" they asked. And the crowds replied, "It's Jesus, the prophet from Nazareth in Galilee." (NLT)

Jesus and the disciples head toward Jerusalem from Bethany. They will soon come over the ridge and take in the breathtaking panorama of the Temple and the surrounding city. Jesus says, "Go into that village, Bethphage, and you'll see a donkey and its colt. Untie them and bring them here. When the people ask what you are doing, tell them that I need them now."

Matthew Henry [COMMENTARY ON THE HOLY BIBLE, MATTHEW – REVELATION] (Matt 21:1-11, last ¶) lays the unshakable cornerstone for a look at why Jesus' disciples simply *obey*. MH first rehearses the testimony of an august list of witnesses:

Moses – *"the seed of the woman, who shall bruise the serpent's head"*

Jacob – *"the Shiloh of the tribe of Judah"*

David – *"the King of glory"*

Isaiah – *"Immanuel, Wonderful, the mighty God, the Prince of peace"*

Jeremiah – *"the righteous Branch"*

Daniel – *"the Messiah"*

John the Baptist – *"the Lamb of God"*

God – *"This is my beloved Son, in whom I am well pleased"*

(even) demons – *"I know thee who thou art, the Holy One of God"*

Then he clearly states the conclusion that anyone immersed in the whole counsel of God will come to: "On no side hath Christ left himself without a full and plain testimony."

As Jesus rode the donkey colt into Jerusalem, Heaven's host was singing so loud that the rocks would have burst into song had not the people joined in. David's expectant song had resonated from the Temple for centuries, *"Hosanna! Blessed is he who comes in the name of the Lord!"* (see Zechariah 9:9 & Psalm 118).

That is what Heaven and the people were shouting. But our purpose here is to hear Jesus' voice as He said to His disciples, *"Go into the town there and you'll see a donkey and its colt. Untie them. The owner will ask what you are doing but just tell him who wants them and bring them here."*

We don't have any narrative for what was going through the minds of the disciples, but the memories of the Psalms and the Prophets had to be at least a subconscious basis for their unquestioning obedience. It is also possible they were a little numb at this point. A lot has happened. For example, Lazarus is back from the dead; repeated warnings that Jesus is going to die; and events are accelerating toward Passover and the sacrifice of the Pesach Lamb of God. Nevertheless, they do what they are told and they help set up the scene. The donkey was a common mode of transportation. It surely didn't speak of the entry of a conquering King. That would require a magnificent stallion. Rather than a conqueror this was the triumphal entry of a judge bringing justice and mercy rather than domination.

Jesus, who created all the people and all the donkeys, and who could have gotten more with a quick, *"Let there be…,"* is actually *asking for help* arranging the transportation for an event. And the event only becomes significant to the disciples when the crowd begins to usher this humble prophet/judge into the city with waving branches and loud cries.

There is one profoundly simple message from this scene. Through natural eyes it would be confusing from just about every point of view. The unavoidable message to the twice-born is, **Jesus knows what He is doing and we don't, but He wants to share *doing it* with us. He is God and we aren't, but He wants to teach us His ways. Therefore, obedience is the only gate through which we may see His perspective, His reasons and His purpose.**

Obedience to what Jesus shows us, is like laying one brick upon another. The picture that He sees is a construction site. The cornerstone must be placed, perfect in every aspect, line and angle. Once that is done, the whole house is built with the understanding that each stone must be laid in perfect alignment to that cornerstone.

All the apostles said in one way or another that we are the "living stones," being built into a house for God. We are His House, His Household, His Body, His Family and the foundational basis for that identification is that we have yielded to be aligned with the Cornerstone of the House, the first stone laid and the last word on the rightness and integrity of every element of the Structure.

John the Baptist tried to refuse to do what Jesus had instructed (the first red letters). John was a man of deep religious convictions and strong opinions, and out of those, he was compelled to say, *"No way! I can't do that."* Jesus' words to John were, *"Let it be this way now, because we should do everything righteousness requires"* (CJB).

That baptism scene was before Jesus was taken into the desert to be tested by the devil; before He healed the lepers and the blind, set the spiritual captives free or raised the dead. Now, back in our current context – the disciples have seen all those miracles. It is close to the completion of Jesus' physical installation as the Cornerstone; and after seeing and hearing all He's done in fulfillment of Scripture, there seems to be very little resistance from those on the A-Team. They are still not seeing the complete picture, but at least they have learned this most pervasively simple wisdom, **just do what Jesus says**.

Chapter Thirty Seven

THE TEMPLE
Matthew 21:12-46

*J*esus entered the Temple and began to drive out all the people buying and selling animals for sacrifice. He knocked over the tables of the money changers and the chairs of those selling doves. He said to them, "The Scriptures declare, 'My Temple will be called a house of prayer,' but you have turned it into a den of thieves!"

The blind and the lame came to him in the Temple, and he healed them. The leading priests and the teachers of religious law saw these wonderful miracles and heard even the children in the Temple shouting, "Praise God for the Son of David."

But the leaders were indignant. They asked Jesus, "Do you hear what these children are saying?"

"Yes," Jesus replied. "Haven't you ever read the Scriptures? For they say, 'You have taught children and infants to give you praise.'" Then he returned to Bethany, where he stayed overnight.

In the morning, as Jesus was returning to Jerusalem, he was hungry, and he noticed a fig tree beside the road. He went over to see if there were any figs, but there were only leaves. Then he said to it, "May you never bear fruit again!" And immediately the fig tree withered up. The disciples were amazed when they saw this and asked, "How did the fig tree wither so quickly?"

Then Jesus told them, "I tell you the truth, if you have faith and don't doubt, you can do things like this and much more. You can even say to this mountain, 'May you be lifted up and thrown into the sea,' and it will happen. You can pray for anything, and if you have faith, you will receive it."

When Jesus returned to the Temple and began teaching, the leading priests and elders came up to him. They demanded, "By what authority are you doing all these things? Who gave you the right?"

"I'll tell you by what authority I do these things if you answer one question," Jesus replied. "Did John's authority to baptize come from heaven, or was it merely human?"

They talked it over among themselves. "If we say it was from heaven, he will ask us why we didn't believe John. But if we say it was merely human, we'll be mobbed because the people believe John was a prophet." So they finally replied, "We don't know."

And Jesus responded, "Then I won't tell you by what authority I do these things. But what do you think about this? A man with two sons told the older boy, 'Son, go out and work in the vineyard today.' The son answered, 'No, I won't go,' but later he changed his mind and went anyway. Then the father told the other son, 'You go,' and he said, 'Yes, sir, I will.' But he didn't go. Which of the two obeyed his father?" They replied, "The first."

Then Jesus explained his meaning: "I tell you the truth, corrupt tax collectors and prostitutes will get into the Kingdom of God before you do. For John the Baptist came and showed you the right way to live, but you didn't believe him, while tax collectors and prostitutes did. And even when you saw this happening, you refused to believe him and repent of your sins.

"Now listen to another story. A certain landowner planted a vineyard, built a wall around it, dug a pit for pressing out the grape juice, and built a lookout tower. Then he leased the vineyard to tenant farmers and moved to another country. At the time of the grape harvest, he sent his servants to collect his share of the crop. But the farmers grabbed his servants, beat one, killed one, and stoned another. So the landowner sent a larger group of his servants to collect for him, but the results were the same.

"Finally, the owner sent his son, thinking, 'Surely they will respect my son.'

"But when the tenant farmers saw his son coming, they said to one another, 'Here comes the heir to this estate. Come on, let's kill him and get the estate for ourselves!' So they grabbed him, dragged him out of the vineyard, and murdered him.

"When the owner of the vineyard returns," Jesus asked, "what do you think he will do to those farmers?"

The religious leaders replied, "He will put the wicked men to a horrible death and lease the vineyard to others who will give him his share of the crop after each harvest."

Then Jesus asked them, "Didn't you ever read this in the Scriptures? 'The stone that the builders rejected has now become the cornerstone. This is the Lord's doing, and it is wonderful to see.' I tell you, the Kingdom of God will be taken away from you and given to a nation that will produce the proper fruit. Anyone who stumbles over that stone will be broken to pieces, and it will crush anyone it falls on."

When the leading priests and Pharisees heard this parable, they realized he was telling the story against them—they were the wicked farmers. They wanted to arrest him, but they were afraid of the crowds, who considered Jesus to be a prophet. (NLT)

#1 (v13) – *"The Scriptures declare..."*
Isaiah 56:7 – *I will bring them also to my holy mountain of Jerusalem and will fill them with joy in my house of prayer. I will accept their burnt offerings and sacrifices, because my Temple will be called a house of prayer for all nations.*
Jeremiah 7:11 – *Do you think this Temple, which honors my name, is a den of thieves? I see all the evil going on there, says the LORD.*

#2 (v16) – *"Haven't you ever read the Scriptures?"*
Psalm 8:2 – *You have taught children and nursing infants to give you praise. They silence your enemies who were seeking revenge.*

#3 (v42) – *"Didn't you ever read this in the Scriptures?"*
Psalm 118:22-23 – *The stone rejected by the builders has now become the cornerstone. This is the LORD's doing, and it is marvelous to see.*
Let's put our explorer's cap on.
Now, concentrate and follow this pattern (**1,2,3**) and connect it with the forensics of our hearts.
The Temple's reputation in God's view:
It is *"Called..."*
#1 - *A place of prayer/healing*
#2 - *A place of praise/rejoicing*
The Temple's design and construction:
#3 – Aligned upon – *The Cornerstone*
Then: Jesus clears the Temple.
Now apply that to what all the apostles said in one way or another:
WE ARE THE TEMPLE.

The disciples had no clue what Jesus was illustrating until the day the Holy Spirit came and began to reveal what His physical Body would look like on earth after He ascended to the right hand of the Father. The Temple meant many things to them, but that it was a pre-view of what God was going to do in each believer, was not one of them.

The house He is building, His house, is to be called (known as) a house of prayer. WE ARE STONES, WE ARE THAT HOUSE.

"*To be called a house of prayer.*" Called – by whom?

At first, it sounds like both Jesus (in Matthew) and God (in Isaiah) are referring to a public reputation. But when we take into consideration the lack of discernment that even "the builders" have (they rejected the Cornerstone, for goodness sake!), we can't assume that the public will ever really have a correct assessment of what's going on. The same lips spoke, "*There's only one good.*" God's assessment is the only one Jesus regards as valid. The house of prayer is us and the One to call us a house of prayer is the only One who would know for sure, our God and Savior, Jesus.

Chapter Thirty Eight

PLEASE RSVP
Matthew 22:1-14

*J*esus also told them other parables. He said, "The Kingdom of Heaven can be illustrated by the story of a king who prepared a great wedding feast for his son. When the banquet was ready, he sent his servants to notify those who were invited. But they all refused to come!

"So he sent other servants to tell them, 'The feast has been prepared. The bulls and fattened cattle have been killed, and everything is ready. Come to the banquet!' But the guests he had invited ignored them and went their own way, one to his farm, another to his business. Others seized his messengers and insulted them and killed them.

"The king was furious, and he sent out his army to destroy the murderers and burn their town. And he said to his servants, 'The wedding feast is ready, and the guests I invited aren't worthy of the honor. Now go out to the street corners and invite everyone you see.' So the servants brought in everyone they could find, good and bad alike, and the banquet hall was filled with guests.

"But when the king came in to meet the guests, he noticed a man who wasn't wearing the proper clothes for a wedding. 'Friend,' he asked, 'how is it that you are here without wedding clothes?' But the man had no reply. Then the king said to his aides, 'Bind his hands and feet and throw him into the outer darkness, where there will be weeping and gnashing of teeth.' "For many are called, but few are chosen." (NLT)

'The wedding feast is ready, and the guests I invited aren't worthy of the honor. Now go out to the street corners and invite everyone you see.' So the servants brought in everyone they could find, good and bad alike, and the banquet hall was filled with guests.

"None are excluded but those who exclude themselves" *(Matthew Henry).*

"Both the city and the country have their temptations, the merchandise in the one, and the farms in the other; so that, whatever we have of the world in our hands, our care must be to keep it out of our hearts, lest it come between us and Christ" *(Matthew Henry).*

With the Words of God there are infinite levels of meaning. Not conflicting meaning, but different levels or angles of application. It reminds me of Star Trek. I can remember being fascinated by the scenes with a couple of the characters playing a chess game that was multilevel. Quite a mutation of the single-level, traditional chess game that we know, which is already intricately complicated. When Jesus speaks, it is certainly that kind of communication, though at the moment He is speaking to us, there is specific application with no question what He means. Each time we read the same Words, hearing Him speak personally to us, there will appear something we have never seen before.

When multi-levels of meaning are in view, we must depend on the panorama of the Book gained by the repeated reading through it [enter the data] and the fact that the Holy Spirit, who dwells inside us, knows Jesus intimately and has the insatiable desire to reveal Him to us. That panorama is the backdrop that tests our interpretations, no matter what level the chess piece may land on.

It seems clear that, with Jesus, there really isn't the distinction of "shallow" or "deep" when it refers to His disclosure of Himself. There is only what He is showing to us now, and how that affects our relationship with Him and the world around us. "Shallow" or "deep" then would only be used to indicate the depth of penetration and transformation we allow in us.

This parable is a simple storyboard, which reveals the motivation and method of God's actions toward humans as history has unfolded. God **so** loved the world – that He wanted to marry it. Even as a kid, we knew that is a lot; up there comparable with loving your puppy or new bike!

Keep this in mind: God has priorities and precedents but they do not constrain Him in reaching His objectives.

He wanted guests for the wedding and had a list. He sent the servants out to gather all on the list. When the invitations were thrown away or rejected by the "A-List," he invited anybody and everybody, the good, the bad and the ugly. Thank You, Jesus!

The story demands a question be answered, in our subconscious if not consciously. That question, "Which am I?" Am I one of the anybodies? Am I one of the A-List? Am I the Bride? There is where the penetration begins. The levels expand and seem to be complicated by multiplied questions and answers. But it is not complicated for God. There is a firm and sure answer. There is an actual winner to the multilevel chess game. Next question, "How do we get there?"

Our attention naturally gravitates to the "unfortunate" soul who becomes the abrupt focus at the end of the story – the one who is brutally expelled. That soul suddenly assumes center-stage and is the example for the lesson, "many, but few."

"The few." We immediately picture the elite, the pros, the top-shelf. But here we have another Sermon-On-The-Mount-type whiplash. The few turn out to be the bottom of the heap, the inept, the amateurs. That revelation thrown into our cultural circuitry is regular and unrelenting in God's Book. *"You have too many, Gideon." "Blessed are the poor." "The powerful lord it over their subjects, but with you..."* Will we ever just get it? *"The greatest among you will be the servant of all." "I came that you might have life."* Real life. Not "marketable" life! Not the life that the world competes for. REAL LIFE. And this is it: the highest value is reached by bowing to the lowest shelf. The REAL joy is granted to those who go to the cross and learn how to surrender in complete faith to the Life that has been delivered to us by the Greatest in the Kingdom.

And, oh yes, we can't afford to forget to wear the clothes He gives us! Our identification is His definitions, perspective and purpose. Our identification is Him in us, our hope of glory, Jesus.

Chapter Thirty Nine

THE FINAL Q&A
Matthew 22:15-46

*T*hen the Pharisees met together to plot how to trap Jesus into saying something for which he could be arrested. They sent some of their disciples, along with the supporters of Herod, to meet with him. "Teacher," they said, "we know how honest you are. You teach the way of God truthfully. You are impartial and don't play favorites. Now tell us what you think about this: Is it right to pay taxes to Caesar or not?"

But Jesus knew their evil motives. "You hypocrites!" he said. "Why are you trying to trap me? Here, show me the coin used for the tax." When they handed him a Roman coin, he asked, "Whose picture and title are stamped on it?"

"Caesar's," they replied.

"Well, then," he said, "give to Caesar what belongs to Caesar, and give to God what belongs to God."

His reply amazed them, and they went away.

That same day Jesus was approached by some Sadducees—religious leaders who say there is no resurrection from the dead. They posed this question: "Teacher, Moses said, 'If a man dies without children, his brother should marry the widow and have a child who will carry on the brother's name.' Well, suppose there were seven brothers. The oldest one married and then died without children, so his brother married the widow. But the second brother also died, and the third brother married her. This continued with all seven of them. Last of all, the woman also died. So tell us, whose wife will she be in the resurrection? For all seven were married to her."

Jesus replied, "Your mistake is that you don't know the Scriptures, and you don't know the power of God. For when the dead rise, they will neither marry nor be given in marriage. In this respect they will be like the angels in heaven. But now, as to whether there will be a resurrection of the dead—haven't you ever read about this in the Scriptures? Long after Abraham, Isaac, and Jacob had died, God said, 'I am the God of Abraham, the God of Isaac, and the God of Jacob.' So he is the God of the living, not the dead."

When the crowds heard him, they were astounded at his teaching.

But when the Pharisees heard that he had silenced the Sadducees with his reply, they met together to question him again. One of them, an expert in religious law, tried to trap him with this question: "Teacher, which is the most important commandment in the law of Moses?"

Jesus replied, "'You must love the Lord your God with all your heart, all your soul, and all your mind.' This is the first and greatest commandment. A second is equally important: 'Love your neighbor as yourself.' The entire law and all the demands of the prophets are based on these two commandments."

Then, surrounded by the Pharisees, Jesus asked them a question: "What do you think about the Messiah? Whose son is he?"

They replied, "He is the son of David."

Jesus responded, "Then why does David, speaking under the inspiration of the Spirit, call the Messiah 'my Lord'? For David said, 'The Lord said to my Lord, Sit in the place of honor at my right hand until I humble your enemies beneath your feet.' Since David called the Messiah 'my Lord,' how can the Messiah be his son?"

No one could answer him. And after that, no one dared to ask him any more questions. (NLT)

There is a definite atmosphere of finality here. Jesus is through with the religious leaders' endless and foolish attempts at putting Him in His place. He's at the end of the time allotted for exposing the damage made by their compromise with their carnal nature and religious pride.

Those who can't stomach hearing Jesus yell abuses and cracking the whip of righteous indignation, may also want to dispense with the ugliness of the cross and unappealing anguish over sin as well as any need for a bloody, universe-upsetting intervention. If those people make it to the Marriage Supper of the Lamb, they might try to enroll as "conscientious objectors" when we line up behind Jesus to carry out His judgment on a world that rejected so great a salvation.

At least that's the way they would feel now. That will change soon. When and if they look into His eyes and sit at that Table with Him and the redeemed, they will be filled completely with Him. Not only filled to overflowing with His gracious, comforting, healing love, but with the full extent of the flaming fire of His love which, on behalf of all those "little ones led astray", will consume those who did the deed.

Yes, it is hard to embrace both the grace and the judgment of God at the same time. That is because we have been duped into believing that they are separate – opposites. That is an evil and pervasive slander, whispered into the ear of every soul who opens God's Book. And the flesh, lusting after its own gratification, too cheaply succumbs and even conspires with the *lie*. The lie is a snarling accusation that starts with, "If God is a loving god, why...?" and then, actually mouthing the words of the father of the *lie*, "Your god is a celestial terrorist!" No. My God is Light and Love, which is a consuming fire that saves, heals AND also wields final vengeance.

Darkness is the absence of light. Cold is the absence of warmth. Love is the absence of self-deifying isolation. God is Love. And that love is righteous and perfect. Jesus has overcome the darkness because He is The Light! There is no darkness in Him and no Shadow of turning. So, what's the problem? Why the need for the cross?

The problem is that God wants fellowship, to enlarge His family with people wholly given to Him and each other; distinct but one, giving and receiving, always and completely for each other. To have that, He had to make human beings – not just beings, but human. He didn't just call into existence a BEING. Angels are of that sort. With angels there is service and loyalty, and a unique extension of God's thoughts and actions, but it seems there is no broad understanding or integration of love, nor capacity for love in the way we are commanded in Scripture.

Part of the nature of our Creator is how He deals with having infinite options. What will He choose and why would He choose that from the infinite choices that God, being infinite, would have? Exactly! So, to have fellowship, to become one with more people in a family, they would have to have choices. They would have to be made in His image, after His nature, so they could freely make the choice to have that fellowship with Him or not.

Character is created by choices and Jesus is the perfect manifestation of the character and disposition of God, seen in human action. His character is flawless with a perfect track record. As humans connected with Him, we discover what Jesus chooses and choose that, so that we can become the gift God wouldn't have unless we chose to give it. There's a lot more choosing going on than we realize.

I would like to get into the difference between what God's choices makes Him and what Satan's choices made him. That's for later. But right there is the first clue to discovering what kind of character we are. We become what we choose, and we can make the choice right now. The

Holy Spirit is present to nudge us toward choosing to personally know God and we, because of all that God has done, can simply say, "okay." It is that action – that choice – which allows the Holy Spirit to begin to show us, teach us and graft us into the God who so loved His creation, "that He sent His Son, so that" if we choose to base our life on that love, we won't perish but will have life bubbling up out of our reconstituted soul from this moment on, to beyond the vanishing point.

Sound like a good deal? Since we are in charge of our choices, give God what belongs to God and don't make the mistake of making conclusions without knowing the Scriptures. Notice how many times Jesus' reply to challenges started with, *"Your mistake is that you don't know the scriptures,"* or, *"Have you not read in scripture ...?"* Jesus' disciples are made through immersion in everything God is, drowned in the pure water of the Word and trained to live it out in every aspect of our daily lives.

Faith, what a simple choice. Just choose with all your heart, mind and strength!

Chapter Forty

HEAVEN'S VIEW OF RELIGIOUS PRIDE
Matthew 23:1-39
[Enter the data.]

*T*HEN JESUS said to the multitudes and to His disciples, "The scribes and Pharisees sit on Moses' seat [of authority]. So observe and practice all they tell you; but do not do what they do, for they preach, but do not practice. They tie up heavy loads, hard to bear, and place them on men's shoulders, but they themselves will not lift a finger to help bear them. They do all their works to be seen of men; for they make wide their phylacteries (small cases enclosing certain Scripture passages, worn during prayer on the left arm and forehead) and make long their fringes [worn by all male Israelites, according to the command]. And they take pleasure in and [thus] love the place of honor at feasts and the best seats in the synagogues, and to be greeted with honor in the marketplaces and to have people call them rabbi."

"But you are not to be called rabbi (teacher), for you have one Teacher and you are all brothers. And do not call anyone [in the church] on earth father, for you have one Father, Who is in heaven. And you must not be called masters (leaders), for you have one Master (Leader), the Christ. He who is greatest among you shall be your servant. Whoever exalts himself [with haughtiness and empty pride] shall be humbled (brought low), and whoever humbles himself [whoever has a modest opinion of himself and behaves accordingly] shall be raised to honor."

"But woe to you, scribes and Pharisees, pretenders (hypocrites)! For you shut the kingdom of heaven in men's faces; for you neither enter yourselves, nor do you allow those who are about to go in to do so. Woe to you, scribes and Pharisees, pretenders (hypocrites)! For you swallow up widows' houses and for a pretense to cover it up make long prayers; therefore you will receive the greater condemnation and the heavier sentence. Woe to you, scribes and Pharisees, pretenders (hypocrites)! For you travel over sea and land to make a single proselyte, and when he becomes one [a proselyte], you make him doubly as much a child of hell (Gehenna) as you are. Woe to you, blind guides, who say, If anyone swears by the sanctuary of the temple, it is nothing; but if anyone swears by the gold of the sanctuary, he is a debtor [bound by his oath]. You blind fools! For which is greater: the gold, or the sanctuary of the temple that has made the gold sacred?"

"You say too, Whoever swears by the altar is not duty bound; but whoever swears by the offering on the altar, his oath is binding. You blind men! Which is greater: the gift, or the altar which makes the gift sacred? So whoever swears by the altar swears by it and by everything on it. And he who swears by the sanctuary of the temple swears by it and by Him Who dwells in it. [see I Kings 8:13; Ps. 26:8.] And whoever swears by heaven swears by the throne of God and by Him Who sits upon it."

"Woe to you, scribes and Pharisees, pretenders (hypocrites)! For you give a tenth of your mint and dill and cummin, and have neglected and omitted the weightier (more important) matters of the Law--right and justice and mercy and fidelity. These you ought [particularly] to have done, without neglecting the others. You blind guides, filtering out a gnat and gulping down a camel!"

"Woe to you, scribes and Pharisees, pretenders (hypocrites)! For you clean the outside of the cup and of the plate, but within they are full of extortion (prey, spoil, plunder) and grasping self-indulgence. You blind Pharisee! First clean the inside of the cup and of the plate, so that the outside may be clean also. Woe to you, scribes and Pharisees, pretenders (hypocrites)! For you are like tombs that have been whitewashed, which look beautiful on the outside but inside are full of dead men's bones and everything impure. Just so, you also outwardly seem to people to be just and upright but inside you are full of pretense and lawlessness and iniquity."

"Woe to you, scribes and Pharisees, pretenders (hypocrites)! For you build tombs for the prophets and decorate the monuments of the righteous, saying, If we had lived in the days of our forefathers, we would not have aided them in shedding the blood of the prophets. Thus you are testifying against yourselves that you are the descendants of those who murdered the prophets. Fill up, then, the measure of your fathers' sins to the brim [so that nothing may be wanting to a full measure]. You serpents! You spawn of vipers! How can you escape the penalty to be suffered in hell (Gehenna)?"

"Because of this, take notice: I am sending you prophets and wise men (interpreters and teachers) and scribes (men learned in the Mosaic Law and the Prophets); some of them you will kill, even crucify, and some you will flog in your synagogues and pursue and persecute from town to town, so that upon your heads may come all the blood of the righteous (those who correspond to the divine standard of right) shed on earth, from the blood of the righteous Abel to the blood of Zechariah son of Barachiah, whom you murdered between the sanctuary and the altar [of burnt offering]. Truly I declare to you, all these [evil, calamitous times] will come upon this generation" (see II Chron. 36:15, 16).

"O Jerusalem, Jerusalem, murdering the prophets and stoning those who are sent to you! How often would I have gathered your children together as a mother fowl gathers her brood under her wings, and you refused! Behold, your house is forsaken and desolate (abandoned and left destitute of God's help) (see I Kings 9:7; Jer. 22:5). *For I declare to you, you will not see Me again until you say, Blessed (magnified in worship, adored, and exalted) is He Who comes in the name of the Lord!"* (AMPC)

Jesus is not just articulating the view and standard of Heaven, He IS the Standard, and not only of Heaven but of all creation as well. Therefore, the Standard now is no longer a law which cannot be attained, a list of divine rules designed to expose our lost and rebellious state. He, the Standard is the Seed from which the Sons of Righteousness are born. Yes, our source code (DNA) has been tampered with, but that tampering was with Man's permission. Right there in the perfect environment of the beauty and fruitfulness that only God could create, the rule exposed what some would call the "weakness" in God's design, Man's sovereign volition. That "weakness" becomes surpassing strength, once Redemption is revealed. That weakness also exposes the nature of the predator who always takes advantage of weakness in the creature in order to malign the Creator. Like a shark to the taste of blood in the water, the serpent is there to devour. But Jesus is also the Stone, not cut with human hands, that will roll down and crush the works of the evil one and draw to Himself those who have overcome him by the Blood of the Lamb and the word of their testimony – those who become His flesh-and-blood Heel which crushes the serpent's head – a divine trap! What a future He has forged for we who have ears to hear and by faith accept the graces which assure that we will share in this Victory of all victories!

Jesus says, "Do what they say, but do not do what they do." There are two very important points He is making.

The first is verified by the history of the Pharisees. Yes, their influence was mixed with "leaven"- pride, avarice and deceit. But history, as well as the language Jesus employs in these scorching rebukes (remember, rebukes come from a caring father, not one that has written off the child), tell us that the Scribes and Pharisees were the guardians of the Torah. Had it not been for their white-hot passion to preserve and interpret the Word of God for His people, we would not have it at our fingertips today. Because of them, we have the first edge of the Living, Two-Edged Sword which does surgery on every soul who is exposed to it. "Do what they say..." was clear confirmation of the veracity of what they faithfully proclaimed from Torah. Then secondly He says, "BUT, beware of their leaven!"

This brings us face to face with the second point: His injunction, "Do not do what they do." This means they (we) are to pay attention and distinguish between what they teach from the Torah, and their life-style, attitude and influence. This expectation, that we can actually make the distinction, is rich with implications. Jesus is not merely suggesting, but commanding, that His disciples should use their wits, which then suggests that they will be able to make the distinction. Also, this whole interaction with the religious leaders clearly shows that we are not to throw out the baby with the dirty bathwater. The common judgment today to a fallen servant of God who has faithfully delivered and interpreted the Word of God is that his teaching is thrown out along with his standing. Jesus is suggesting that we have a larger spirit than that, His Spirit. So through faith in His Spirit, we can both discern the wisdom to distinguish **and** apply the grace of God. Jesus was clearly not throwing out the teaching. **And,** though the rebuke was stinging, His love and grace toward them were the motives behind the warning.

PRIME CHALLENGE

We must be careful not to make the mistake of deifying our own perspective, presuming it is insight into God's Word. Our natural perspectives are programmed by a world of experience outside of God's Reality. We must attain to the stature of the fullness of Yeshua. From that base, we can have deep fellowship in our relationships, with the responsible intellect and capacity for relevant conversation; walking, thinking, talking from our base in Him. There are clear earmarks of deifying our point of view and they are all revealed in what happens to relationships among Jesus' Body-parts. It is time well spent to search them out in the apostles' letters dealing with that in the first-century churches.

May I point to several scriptures that will help this scene become intimately personal to we who read it over and over? I pray that Jesus' points sink deeply into our crusty and self-justifying hearts so we will not glibly read through His words, but passionately seek after Him and His perspective. His words are alive and powerful to the pulling down of strongholds – the dulling barriers in our own hearts.

Isaiah 55:6-9 *"Seek the Lord while he may be found; call upon him while he is near; let the wicked forsake his way, and the unrighteous man his thoughts; let him return to the Lord, that he may have compassion on him, and to our God, for he will abundantly pardon. For my thoughts are not your thoughts, neither are your ways my ways, declares the Lord."*

Proverbs 13:10, 26:20-21
1Corinthians 1,3,6,11
Philippians 2
Colossians 3
2Timothy 2
James 4

Chapter Forty One

ME & TIME

At this point, it is crucial to address *how* we read what Jesus is saying, and for that matter, *how* we read all Scripture.

Our illusion of time can be a distraction from the work of diligently looking for Jesus and hearing what He says. We must establish in our minds that God is not bound by our perspective and understanding. He especially designed and created all that this world includes, an environment in which *WE* can live, discover and grow. It is His elaborate incubator, to hatch beings from the shell of an isolated bubble-world, to be His intimate friends and integrated extensions of His infinite being throughout eternity. That means we cannot perceive *His* perspective or understand *His* thoughts based on *our* perspective or *our* thoughts. He is holy, *so* outside this world He created for our training, that He likens it, in Isaiah 55, to the difference between the ground you stand on and the extreme extent of the Cosmos. That means the two cannot possibly be related, until His revelation of Himself becomes our identity. We need to practice making that clear to ourselves every time we open His Book. He is speaking to us from outside our little reality to transform us by the reconstruction of our minds, giving us glimpses and tastes of the world we were born for. Be a reminder to each other - This life is just the qualifying round for the perpetual Main Event!

This issue of time is a very fascinating one. There is no use trying to nail it down. Yet there are a lot of people who are so obsessed with it that they assume the authority to dictate to their whole environment, people and situations alike, based on their assumption that time is somehow a static, solid boundary. Nowhere in history or even as we progress in scientific knowledge and technology has Man been able to define or confine time. Even Bible scholars seem to miss the glaring fact that the narrative of God's revelation of Himself contains only vague designations of time. The historical record, something to be taken in a sort of time-line, includes such phrases as, "In the beginning"; "In the third year of Ahab's reign;" and "a time, times and a half time." When that record is resumed after the "blank" years in the writings of the Apostles, there are even less clear designations. The modern translators have calculated the references against historical calendars and throughout the whole Book interjected the approximate date accordingly.

All that is said to shake us loose from our obsession with "what we think we know," so that we might discern God's perspective in the text we are reading. When that thought first dawns in our mind, we are powerfully stricken with the terror that while reading His Holy Word we might be drowning out the voice of the Holy Spirit – God's very voice – with our own assumptions and calculations. Then, we remember that He has said in clear language to us, "*If you ask for wisdom, I'm right there ready to give it*" (see James 1:5). We are also reminded that if we are reading along with ears to hear, asking for wisdom, the Holy Spirit will have the prerogative to arrest our attention and pull us into His confidence.

Hear Jesus' voice as He says to us, "*Don't be afraid.*" And then hear Paul's exposition of the Spirit's answer to our blank-staring question, "**Why ever not?**" "*For [because] God did not give us a spirit of timidity or cowardice or fear, but [He has given us a spirit] of power and of love and of sound judgment and personal discipline [abilities that result in a calm, well-balanced mind and self-control]* (2Timothy 1:7 AMP). That gift from Him releases us to be boldly following the direction of His eye, hearing the intimate whispers of His Spirit, and to joyfully respond and follow Him with our whole heart, mind, soul and strength.

This life is really wonderful, if we are able to practice this **loose-grip/easy-return-to-sanity** dance with the Holy Spirit, and persistently work toward letting go completely. Instead of nailing our illusions down, let them be absorbed into the continuity of God's communication to us. These disciple-making Jesus-Words that transformed Matthew into His disciple, are a key for anyone who would be Jesus' disciple. If we are not able to let go, we will be bogged down in trying to get the, "When is that?" and "Wait! Which time is that?" questions worked out, like the disciples would have been doing until the Counselor was given to them on Pentecost. That is when they were changed from Jesus' disciples [talmidim] to His friends, because all the questions were suddenly either answered or settled by the present reality of His Spirit in them. And, by the way, they didn't have Matthew's

Gospel to go back to and read the account again. What they did have was the "*Counselor, the Spirit of Truth, Who will teach you all things and bring to your remembrance all that I have spoken to you.*" AH! That'll do!

If you have gotten to this point in our recall of the Jesus-Words, there's a good chance that He, the same Holy Spirit, is in you. So, when you read His Book, hear what the correspondence of God's Word, made living flesh, is saying to *you*. Just let it have its rightful place in your heart as the data is entered and the Holy Spirit whispers His insight; and depend on Him to bring it to your remembrance and to give you the childlike spontaneity to boldly apply it to the situation in which He has put you, this minute. He designed everything, yes everything to be synchronized for our good in every tick of His enormous clock, the universe. Our job is to keep entering the data and getting better at hearing what Jesus is saying, aligning our heart and mind with His, rather than arranging it into a clever little palatable dogma. What He says transforms us moment to moment, glimpse to glimpse, glory to glory.

Chapter Forty Two

GOD'S TIMING, MARKED BY MOMENTOUS ENCOUNTERS
Matthew 24

[Recommended: Read through as written aloud.
Absorb the continuity of the events.]

*T*ruly I tell you, there will not be left here one stone upon another that will not be thrown down.

Tell us, when will this take place, and what will be the sign of Your coming and of the end of the age?

Be careful that no one misleads you [deceiving you and leading you into error]. ...many will come in (on the strength of) My name [appropriating the name which belongs to Me], saying, I am the Christ (the Messiah), and they will lead many astray.

...nation will rise against nation, and kingdom against kingdom, and there will be famines and earthquakes in place after place; All this is but the beginning [the early pains] of the birth pangs [of the intolerable anguish].

... they will hand you over to suffer affliction and tribulation and put you to death, and you will be hated by all nations for My name's sake.

... many will be offended and repelled and will begin to distrust and desert [Him Whom they ought to trust and obey] and will stumble and fall away and betray one another and pursue one another with hatred.

... many false prophets will rise up and deceive and lead many into error.

... the love of the great body of people will grow cold because of the multiplied lawlessness and iniquity, But he who endures to the end will be saved.

... this good news of the kingdom (the Gospel) will be preached throughout the whole world as a testimony to all the nations, and then *will come the end.*

... just as the lightning flashes from the east and shines and is seen as far as the west, so will the coming of the Son of Man be. Immediately after the tribulation of those days the sun will be darkened

... the moon will not shed its light

... the stars will fall from the sky

... the powers of the heavens will be shaken

... the sign of the Son of Man will appear in the sky

... all the tribes of the earth will mourn and beat their breasts and lament in anguish, and they will see the Son of Man coming on the clouds of heaven with power and great glory [in brilliancy and splendor].

... He will send out His angels with a loud trumpet call

... they will gather His elect (His chosen ones) from the four winds, [even] from one end of the universe to the other.

... when you see these signs, all taken together, coming to pass, you may know of a surety that He is near, at the very doors.

... As were the days of Noah, so will be the coming of the Son of Man.

... just as in those days before the flood they were eating and drinking, [men] marrying and [women] being given in marriage, until the [very] day when Noah went into the ark, and they did not know or understand until the flood came and swept them all away--so will be the coming of the Son of Man.

... two men will be in the field; one will be taken and one will be left.

... Two women will be grinding at the hand mill; one will be taken and one will be left.

... Watch therefore [give strict attention, be cautious and active], for you do not know in what kind of a day [whether a near or remote one] your Lord is coming.

... be ready therefore, for the Son of Man is coming at an hour when you do not expect Him.

...Who then is the faithful, thoughtful, and wise servant, whom his master has put in charge of his household to give to the others the food and supplies at the proper time?

... Blessed (happy, fortunate, and to be envied) is that servant whom, when his master comes, he will find so doing. I solemnly declare to you, he will set him over all his possessions.

... But if that servant is wicked and says to himself, my master is delayed and is going to be gone a long time, and begins to beat his

fellow servants and to eat and drink with the drunken, the master of that servant will come on a day when he does not expect him and at an hour of which he is not aware, and will punish him [cut him up by scourging] and put him with the pretenders (hypocrites); there will be weeping and grinding of teeth. (AMPC)

TICK! TOCK! TICK! TOCK!

These are moments of encounter that mark God's timing, marks of progress toward the completion of the blueprinted goal of this age. "As in the day of Noah." Each moment begs the urgent question - Are we inside? Are we safe? Have we heard and obeyed the call to get inside? Have we? Jesus goes through the marks on God's timetable with the undisguised goal of installing the terrifying thrill of God into the hearts of His disciples. He is doing that as we read His words, so we will get the reality embedded in our hearts and minds that the Son of Man is coming for us and we must be ready and busy about His business!

Every time we read, "In the beginning..." or "In the year..." or "In the 8th year of Josiah's reign..." or "Truly I tell you...," we mark it. Not the exact date, but mark and take note of what happened. Who was having the encounter and how did they respond? "In the year that King Uziah died," what happened? No need to fuss with the exact date or time. The scientists say that the universe is one giant clock. By being immersed in His Book, we discover what makes God's clock tick, with the full determination to get inside the point of each particular encounter in the passage being read. Just take them one at a time, as they come. God has designed even the sequence so that it will draw us and transform us step-by-step to the restoration of our mind. That transformation will clearly mean that we will very likely become crazy in the eyes of the world, but actually, we will be resolutely stepping toward becoming normal for the first time in our lives!

Now clearly, Jesus starts this explanation with what the disciples were personally going to see and experience. The Temple would be literally taken apart, stone by stone. Of this group of twelve, some would live to see that happen in 70 AD. After that, Jesus' view of the disciples blurred as His focus extended beyond them. He saw *us* and all future generations. He described the nightmare in store for the planet in future history. That focus pivoted on the admonition to "be ready," so that is the message to us who hear or read His words. For us to be ready includes all the effect His resurrection had on those first disciples, which caused them to rejoice at the honor to suffer for His name.

Prior to the destruction of the temple in 70 AD, they would go through most people's worst nightmare, but how did they handle those encounters? They rejoiced when they suffered for the name of their Lord. While walking with Jesus during those 3 years of His earthly ministry, they watched Him handle the worst the world and the devil could do to Him. They watched Him be tortured and crucified, *exactly as He had said.* Shrinking behind closed doors they thought the grand idea was crushed and the same people who killed their leader would be coming for them. But then they saw Him, touched Him and talked with Him after He rose from the dead, *just as He had said.* They watched Him ascend into Heaven, *just as He had said.*

Though He had told them the horrors that would be inflicted on them, they were no longer afraid. Now, with a completely revised perspective, they stepped toward the mission for which, in just a few days, the Holy Spirit would equip and empower them. They knew the worst that could happen to them was not that they might suffer and die, but that they might NOT follow their Lord through the cross to His resurrection life. Jesus had led the way on a path that was now open to the whole world and they were going to make sure the whole world heard about it.

Our hearts can be just as filled with the reality of our LIVING Savior for the same reason – we have His Spirit, His very person with us, even in us! He has told us the worst the world can do to us and the judgment coming upon this planet. Now, given our utterly altered identification – no longer OF this world, but completely OF the Cross and our resurrected Lord – we live and walk in His resurrection life. The question, "How shall we then live?" is answered. Jesus lives in me. His life is my life. What we are yet to discover is – "How shall we then die?" We will die daily, surrendering our claim to our right to our self; and rejoicing, no matter what the physical or emotional consequences. We will walk through them in the full, rich joy of our salvation and deep honor to be part of His flesh-and-blood, out-loud and visible Body walking where He puts us and interacting with the people He wants to interact with - in our skin.

His Body has become a beautiful, living and moving filigree net covering the face of earth – His human flesh-and-blood boots on the ground. His physical hands are holding this planet, calling and wooing it toward its Designer, Creator, Father, Redeemer and Lord who SO LOVED!

Each encounter marks God's time. Each one brings us closer to seeing Him face to Face! Soon and Very Soon! MARANATHA!

Chapter Forty Three

IN OR OUT?
Matthew 25

*T*HEN THE kingdom of heaven shall be likened to ten virgins who took their lamps and went to meet the bridegroom. Five of them were foolish (thoughtless, without forethought) and five were wise (sensible, intelligent, and prudent). For when the foolish took their lamps, they did not take any [extra] oil with them; But the wise took flasks of oil along with them [also] with their lamps.

While the bridegroom lingered and was slow in coming, they all began nodding their heads, and they fell asleep. But at midnight there was a shout, Behold, the bridegroom! Go out to meet him! Then all those virgins got up and put their own lamps in order. And the foolish said to the wise, Give us some of your oil, for our lamps are going out. But the wise replied, There will not be enough for us and for you; go instead to the dealers and buy for yourselves. But while they were going away to buy, the bridegroom came, and those who were prepared went in with him to the marriage feast; and the door was shut. Later the other virgins also came and said, Lord, Lord, open [the door] to us! But He replied, I solemnly declare to you, I do not know you [I am not acquainted with you].

Watch therefore [give strict attention and be cautious and active], for you know neither the day nor the hour when the Son of Man will come.

For it is like a man who was about to take a long journey, and he called his servants together and entrusted them with his property. To one he gave five talents [probably about $5,000], to another two, to another one--to each in proportion to his own personal ability. Then he departed and left the country.

He who had received the five talents went at once and traded with them, and he gained five talents more. And likewise he who had received the two talents--he also gained two talents more. But he who had received the one talent went and dug a hole in the ground and hid his master's money.

Now after a long time the master of those servants returned and settled accounts with them. And he who had received the five talents came and brought him five more, saying, Master, you entrusted to me five talents; see, here I have gained five talents more. His master said to him, Well done, you upright (honorable, admirable) and faithful servant! You have been faithful and trustworthy over a little; I will put you in charge of much. Enter into and share the joy (the delight, the blessedness) which your master enjoys. And he also who had the two talents came forward, saying, Master, you entrusted two talents to me; here I have gained two talents more. His master said to him, Well done, you upright (honorable, admirable) and faithful servant! You have been faithful and trustworthy over a little; I will put you in charge of much. Enter into and share the joy (the delight, the blessedness) which your master enjoys.

He who had received one talent also came forward, saying, Master, I knew you to be a harsh and hard man, reaping where you did not sow, and gathering where you had not winnowed [the grain]. So I was afraid, and I went and hid your talent in the ground. Here you have what is your own. But his master answered him, You wicked and lazy and idle servant! Did you indeed know that I reap where I have not sowed and gather [grain] where I have not winnowed? Then you should have invested my money with the bankers, and at my coming I would have received what was my own with interest. So take the talent away from him and give it to the one who has the ten talents. For to everyone who has will more be given, and he will be furnished richly so that he will have an abundance; but from the one who does not have, even what he does have will be taken away. And throw the good-for-nothing servant into the outer darkness; there will be weeping and grinding of teeth.

When the Son of Man comes in His glory (His majesty and splendor), and all the holy angels with Him, then He will sit on the throne of His glory. All nations will be gathered before Him, and He will separate them [the people] from one another as a shepherd separates his sheep from the goats; And He will cause the sheep to stand at His right hand, but the goats at His left.

Then the King will say to those at His right hand, Come, you blessed of My Father [you favored of God and appointed to eternal salvation], inherit (receive as your own) the kingdom prepared for you from the foundation of the world. For I was hungry and you gave

Me food, I was thirsty and you gave Me something to drink, I was a stranger and you brought Me together with yourselves and welcomed and entertained and lodged Me, I was naked and you clothed Me, I was sick and you visited Me with help and ministering care, I was in prison and you came to see Me.

Then the just and upright will answer Him, Lord, when did we see You hungry and gave You food, or thirsty and gave You something to drink? And when did we see You a stranger and welcomed and entertained You, or naked and clothed You? And when did we see You sick or in prison and came to visit You?

And the King will reply to them, Truly I tell you, in so far as you did it for one of the least [in the estimation of men] of these My brethren, you did it for Me. Then He will say to those at His left hand, begone from Me, you cursed, into the eternal fire prepared for the devil and his angels! For I was hungry and you gave Me no food, I was thirsty and you gave Me nothing to drink, I was a stranger and you did not welcome Me and entertain Me, I was naked and you did not clothe Me, I was sick and in prison and you did not visit Me with help and ministering care. Then they also [in their turn] will answer, Lord, when did we see You hungry or thirsty or a stranger or naked or sick or in prison, and did not minister to You?

And He will reply to them, Solemnly I declare to you, in so far as you failed to do it for the least [in the estimation of men] of these, you failed to do it for Me. Then they will go away into eternal punishment, but those who are just and upright and in right standing with God into eternal life. (AMPC)

Following on the contrast of wicked vs. wise servants, extolling the blessedness in store for the latter, Jesus expounds on the nature of the Kingdom of God. His illustrations, "*it will be like,*" give insight into how the contrast between slothful and faithful disposition will ultimately be played out, and then be separated to go to their very different eternal futures.

This section of Scripture contains some of Jesus' best known illustrations – The Ten Virgins & The Bridegroom, The Invested Talents & The Rewards, and The Sheep & The Goats. Of course, the last one of the three is not really about animals. He refers to these creatures because the parallel would be very familiar in that culture and also because, though similar, these animals are easily distinguishable.

The illustration quickly becomes very personal; from "Jesus sits on His Throne and all _nations_ are brought before Him" to "He separates the _people_ as a shepherd separates sheep from goats" (mutton from chevon, wool from hair). That calls to mind the story of the wheat and tares (see Matthew 13). Both thrive in the same _"field,"_ but here in Chapter 25, Jesus is bringing the illustration right up in our laps. _"All nations"_ and _"people"_ means you and me, grown on the same planet. But we are different in one vital respect – our relation to Jesus.

Jesus describes the nature of that relationship in very specific terms – _He_ needed something and _we_ either gave Him what _He_ needed or _we_ didn't.

> "I was:
> Hungry – you fed me, or you didn't
> Thirsty – you gave me a drink, or you didn't
> A stranger – you welcomed me, or you didn't
> Naked – you clothed me, or you didn't
> Sick and in prison – you visited me, or you didn't"

The first thing that strikes me is that He needed something.... _from me._ The next thing is that neither group recognized Him as the one who was in need.

This is quite mysterious. Is it a trick? A test cloaked in disguise? I don't think so. If it were a deception, it wouldn't be Jesus. The problem is not that He was in disguise. The problem is our perception. But here's the kicker – our bad eyesight or mindless oblivion to reality, is not the issue that is being rewarded or punished here. The issue is that we did or did not give Jesus what He needed, whether we recognized Him or not.

Of course, if they had recognized that the needy person was Jesus, they would have given Him what He needed, right? Okay, I know this is jumping off into very deep waters here, but scripture shows that what a person is, is what a person is. In other words, unless the atonement of God through His Messiah's death and resurrection has been applied, there is no transformation in people. People can act differently, but they aren't different. They are just acting. In this context, we are either a giver or we are not – the "good eye"[generous] or the "bad eye"[stingy]. Furthermore, the giver Jesus is describing is the same one that James, the first head of the church in Jerusalem, described in his epistle and called it _"true religion."_

The scary thing about this whole scene is that everybody but Jesus seemed to be oblivious to what was happening. All it is saying to us is, please make sure Jesus is given the prerogative to live out His perception and disposition through us more fully every day. How do we do that? Walk with Him where He puts us, and say what He's saying when we open our mouths. *Take* every thought captive to the nature, the disposition of the Supreme Champion Giver, Savior, the sanity available to us – JESUS. The Point? He and I can see the mark of His image in every person and we know what they need. *"Do not prevent the little children from coming to Me!"* His *"come"* - our lips.

Chapter Forty Four

AND PETER REMEMBERED
Matthew 26

[Only red-letter verses for continuity of Jesus' stream of thought.]

²You know that the Passover is in two days--and the Son of Man will be delivered up treacherously to be crucified.

¹⁰ ... Why do you bother the woman? She has done a noble (praiseworthy and beautiful) thing to Me. ¹¹For you always have the poor among you, but you will not always have Me. ¹²In pouring this perfume on My body she has done something to prepare Me for My burial. ¹³Truly I tell you, wherever this good news (the Gospel) is preached in the whole world, what this woman has done will be told also, in memory of her.

¹⁸ ... Go into the city to a certain man and say to him, The Master says: My time is near; I will keep the Passover at your house with My disciples.

²¹ ... Solemnly I say to you, one of you will betray Me!

²³ ... He who has [just] dipped his hand in the same dish with Me will betray Me!

²⁴ The Son of Man is going just as it is written of Him; but woe to that man by whom the Son of Man is betrayed! It would have been better (more profitable and wholesome) for that man if he had never been born!

²⁵ ... You have stated [the fact].

²⁶ ... Take, eat; this is My body.

²⁷ ... Drink of it, all of you;

²⁸ For this is My blood of the new covenant, which [ratifies the agreement and] is being poured out for many for the forgiveness of sins.

²⁹ I say to you, I shall not drink again of this fruit of the vine until that day when I drink it with you new and of superior quality in My

Father's kingdom.

³¹ ... You will all be offended and stumble and fall away because of Me this night [distrusting and deserting Me], for it is written, I will strike the Shepherd, and the sheep of the flock will be scattered. ³²But after I am raised up [to life again], I will go ahead of you to Galilee.

³⁴ ... Solemnly I declare to you, this very night, before a single rooster crows, you will deny and disown Me three times.

³⁶ ... Sit down here while I go over yonder and pray.

³⁸ ... My soul is very sad and deeply grieved, so that I am almost dying of sorrow. Stay here and keep awake and keep watch with Me.

³⁹ ... My Father, if it is possible, let this cup pass away from Me; nevertheless, not what I will [not what I desire], but as You will and desire.

⁴⁰ ... What! Are you so utterly unable to stay awake and keep watch with Me for one hour? ⁴¹All of you must keep awake (give strict attention, be cautious and active) and watch and pray, that you may not come into temptation. The spirit indeed is willing, but the flesh is weak.

⁴² ... My Father, if this cannot pass by unless I drink it, Your will be done.

⁴⁵ ... Are you still sleeping and taking your rest? Behold, the hour is at hand, and the Son of Man is betrayed into the hands of especially wicked sinners [whose way or nature it is to act in opposition to God].

⁵⁰ ... Friend, for what are you here?

⁵² ... Put your sword back into its place, for all who draw the sword will die by the sword. ⁵³Do you suppose that I cannot appeal to My Father, and He will immediately provide Me with more than twelve legions [more than 80,000] of angels? ⁵⁴But how then would the Scriptures be fulfilled, that it must come about this way?

⁵⁵ ... Have you come out with swords and clubs as [you would] against a robber to capture Me? Day after day I was accustomed to sit in the porches and courts of the temple teaching, and you did not arrest Me. ⁵⁶But all this has taken place in order that the Scriptures of the prophets might be fulfilled.

⁶⁴ ... You have stated [the fact]. More than that, I tell you: You will in the future see the Son of Man seated at the right hand of the Almighty and coming on the clouds of the sky.

⁷⁵ And Peter remembered Jesus' words, Before a single rooster crows, you will deny and disown Me three times. And he went outside and wept bitterly. (AMPC)

And Peter remembered Jesus' words.

Can you imagine the tender compassion of Levi [Matthew], as he wrote in his journal these words about his beloved fellow disciple, Peter?

Jesus is always saying what is real. He is always revealing Himself. That is the heart of God – Father, Son, Holy Ghost. Always completely open, pouring out their brilliance and power on behalf of each other. This is the nature of the One God who created us, who we know and will endlessly discover. His express purpose is to reveal Himself to us and for us.

Why? Because He alone knows what we were made to be, and what we shall be. There is only one "if." **If**, we will remember Him – Jesus' words. If we but give Him the honor He is due, *that* is what makes the whole world go round. It makes the whole mechanism, His whole creation work perfectly, including especially, our hearts.

WHEN WE ACKNOWLEDGE HIM, that is when we taste that perfection. It is only in those supernatural moments of normality, in this age, in these bodies, that give us deep confirmation that His promise is sure. Those supernatural moments of normality are the moments we COMMUNE with Him and He with us... the moments we are WITH HIM. Those are the only moments we are actually alive. So, if you add those up, none of us would really be very old... yet.

Tasted of that heavenly normality today? Determined to make that moment the cornerstone of every day and to have a "life-bath" immersion in "comm-union-cation" with our Father? If so, *we are* that flesh-and-blood-presence of His Son, through which His Spirit is pouring, shining and salting the atmosphere of every room we walk into, every conversation, and every family hug. He is in every move we make and every breath we take. He is speaking through our lips, and giving through our hands things that are beyond our reach, unless He is with us and in us, with full access to our faculties.

These red letters reveal the final stage of human interaction as Jesus navigates across the break-line of history, when God tore through all the barriers and opened the way to extreme and complete communion with Man. For that deep communion with Man, Jesus, begotten expressly for this purpose, alone penetrated the core of enemy territory and took possession of what He had just bought with His blood. He is the perfect cornerstone, upon which His eternal Household is being built with living stones.

The striking feature of Jesus' interaction with the world is that He alone knows what is really happening. The Words He spoke into the disciples and the world, prior to the arrival of *"The Other, Who will bring everything I've said to your remembrance,"* were His installations in the people who would become His flesh-and-blood-presence, multiplying until He would walk and live in every part of the world clothed in human skin.

There is no other life. We are either alive in Him and He in us, or we are not really alive. Have we heard what Jesus is saying to us and reminding ourselves what He has been saying all along? Unless we remember and acknowledge that it is His words that are our food, His water we drink and His air we breath, we would too easily forget that He likes to engage us in conversation – life-transforming conversation. Does it still require the pain of humiliating shame and regret for us to remember He is talking to us? He's still recommending the same cure for all of that. "Go [out of what you think is normal] and wait on My Table, intensely give attention to My needs, My desires [your new normal]. I will send My Spirit to dwell in you and empower you, not only to 'remember My Words,' but to be My flesh-&-blood-Presence, My Life, transforming darkness into Light, despair into peace, wherever you go."

You are where He has sent you. Just take a moment and remember that what He has said to you is meant to be a conversation.

Respond. Talk to Him.

Chapter Forty Five

YOU SAY SO
Matthew 27:11-14

*N*ow Jesus stood before the governor, and the governor asked him, "Are you the King of the Jews?" Jesus said, "You have said so." But when he was accused by the chief priests and elders, he gave no answer. Then Pilate said to him, "Do you not hear how many things they testify against you?" But he gave him no answer, not even to a single charge, so that the governor was greatly amazed. (ESV)

Dig for treasure with me...

Cosmos: *beautiful order; created order; a closed equation; a whole, beyond the comprehension of the individual parts.* That's Jesus' point. What Jesus has created, Cosmos, is beyond the comprehension of us, the individual parts, but... No matter how the experiments and calculations of the parts are done or what conclusions are reached, they all ultimately illustrate and prove the *order.* *"You have said so."* We, the individual parts [Pilate for example] cannot comprehend the whole, but we are part of the whole closed equation, so everything we do confirms and proves it. Whatever our perspective or conclusions, we are only proving a changeless point – God's Creation.

To the mind determined to be independent, this kind of talk is perhaps unbearable, but in the mist of the inevitable frustrated question, "Are You the King?" the calmest, most settled voice ever heard whispers, *"You say so."* No matter what we think or do, we can only prove the inevitable Reality.

> *No matter what knots and twists*
> *We add to the tapestry,*
> *They only add to the texture*
> *And wonder of the Design.*
> *The alive, dancing, graphic message*
> *Suspended across the swirling*
> *Black hole, vacuum of souls.*
> *The light from penetrating, unapproachable*
> *Bursts, through the infinitely varied*
> *Colors of the Creator poured*
> *Into the laser lenses of the created,*
> *Becomes the Salty light for the world.*

How am I responding to that? That's a very important question to ask.

Hitting the natural mind's brick wall between the concepts of the complete sovereignty of God and the volition (sovereignty) of Man, and trying to appease the apparent insoluble conflict between the two, may cause us, like many in the church, to take the position that it is not in anyone's interest to bring the subjects up in the same context. When put on the spot, they disguise their non-proliferation with some intellectual-sounding platitude, which reveals the non-reality of their non-motivation, "I just can't go there." No matter how we may be motivated, Man cannot have one without the other. They are One Point, One Subject, One Concept – in the Mind of God. He is One – THE ONE.

Sh'ma Yis'ra'eil Adonai Eloheinu Adonai echad
(Deuteronomy 6:4-9).
Hear, oh Israel, the Lord is our God, the Lord is One.

The problem with the "I can't go there" position? It is not a position at all. In fact, it reveals that our own conclusion, on any subject, is still the ascendant authority in our own double-mind, which, by definition, blocks the Holy Spirit's work of transforming us by "the renewal of our mind" which means – we prefer to be independent of God's logic, especially when the Holy Spirit is saying something foreign to our way of thinking, or not thinking, in this case (see Rom 12:2, Ephesians 4:23).

This renewal work of the Holy Spirit is showcased during the Feast of Pentecost by the ecstatic proclamation of the attributes of God, spoken by the Ruach HaKodesh [Holy Spirit] through the disciples in

171

each of the startled bystander's language. Not only was the Window of Heaven opened to each disciple, but all were enraptured by the View and Company. Their natural reflex was to become, quite unintentionally, the direct messengers of that Reality in human language. That is the precise definition of the "Glory of God," God's Person and Reality conveyed through human beings, to human beings, in the natural world. Not necessarily by the human's determination, for example: "I'm now going to be the purveyor of the Glory of God," he said, as he swaggered to the sacred desk. *Not*! But a human's spontaneously articulated expression during personal interaction with God and all that is going on around Him, opens a portal and pours a glimpse of Him into the natural world.

Yes, it is impossible for us to process the whole view of God. We are only able to see and understand what He reveals to us. What He is pouring in, is then to be poured out, without extracting elements that make no sense to us. The filter for that spontaneity is simply the childlike being He would make of us, rather than an independent analytical manager of information. He is the one output from our lives that is most valuable when constrained and checked by nothing but what He has already revealed in the continuity of His Word.

"Pilate, everything you are and do answers the question, 'Am I the King of the Jews?' Yes... King, Maker and Savior of the Jews – and of the World. YOU and all you do confirms that."

Chapter Forty Six

GOD-FORSAKEN?
Matthew 27:46,50

*A*nd about the ninth hour Jesus cried out with a loud voice, saying, "Eli, Eli lema sabachthani?" that is, "My God, my God,
why have you forsaken me?"

*And Jesus cried out again with a loud voice and yielded up his
spirit.* (ESV)

A loud, searching call, reverberated through the Universe, "*My God!*" No answer. "*My God!!*"... the desperate cry of a Son who had never known a moment without the intertwined companionship of His Father, abruptly aware of His absence.

In the hollow vacuum of silence, His flesh broken, pierced, and His blood pouring from those voluntary wounds, "*Why?*" comes from the parched lips of the Promised One, the Son of God. "*Why have you forsaken me?*"

Alone, cut off from the Father, there's no logic, no reason for much of anything *for anyone*. Separation from Him is separation from life, reality. For Yeshua the Messiah (actually for all of us), it is like a fish taken from the water – impossible to get a breath. God is not just the provider of our breath. God IS our breath. Since being ejected from the Garden, Man has been born separated from that intimacy, which is anything **but** normal, from Heaven's perspective. From Man's view, isolated is normal, the way it has always been. Jesus is coming from **normal**, the enmeshed life lived for each other[1], to our isolated illusion of life, alone with only self.

He became sin. Sin is defined in the dictionary as an action which violates God's moral law and in turn alienates a human being from God. *Sin*, as defined in the Bible, *is* the isolation, not just an act that causes alienation. Sin is *any* disunion from God. We were born separated from the spiritual Life that makes us a person. Our broken-off, isolated,

Individuality is not part of Personality. Individuality is the absence of Personality, as darkness is the absence of light.

Jesus was not born separated from God's spirit. But, taking on the form of man, *"he learned obedience through what he suffered."* (Hebrews 5:8 ESV), *"one who in every respect has been tempted as we are, yet without sin"* (Hebrews 4:15 ESV). The father was ever present to train and discipline even with the help of others in the cultural environment of a devout Hebrew family, as would any Jewish boy of that day. Jesus heard the history of God's interaction with the chosen people and discovered His own identity, *His own personality,* in the confirmations of the Tanakh, God's oral and written Word.

It is naturally difficult for us to grasp having unbroken intimacy with God and still having to learn obedience through disciplinary training, but that is exactly why the Holy Spirit was to be given to Man from the beginning. Jesus was a human baby and baby boys must become mature men, no matter who their parents might be, and that takes a godly, biblically-functioning family's undivided attentive love and training.

Jesus, here at the finish of His task, even with His impassioned cries echoing through creation, His Father's voice could not be heard. His presence could not be felt. This was the moment that had filled Jesus with crushing dread. The Comm-Union that had always been, was broken. Oh, the unfathomable depths of the love of God, to send His pure Son of promise into the blackhole of Man's dark isolation! This is the pivot-point of Time-Space Creation: sin taken on by the only one who could deal with it personally, and for all eternity wear the title "Lamb of God".

WHY HAVE YOU FORSAKEN ME?

Why? Because the Father loves you and me. He wants an eternity with those who love Him. But how? There is only one Way. He laid His life down for us. He came into our spiritually comatose world, connected the Holy Ghost jumper cables and jump-started our lives.

He who did not withhold or spare [even] His own Son but gave Him up for us all (Romans 8:32a AMPC).

Come and let us return to the Lord, for He has torn so that He may heal us; He has stricken so that He may bind us up (Hosea 6:1 AMPC).

He was despised and rejected—
a man of sorrows, acquainted with deepest grief.
We turned our backs on him and looked the other way.
He was despised, and we did not care.
Yet it was our weaknesses he carried;
it was our sorrows that weighed him down.
And we thought his troubles were a punishment from God,
a punishment for his own sins!
But he was pierced for our rebellion,
crushed for our sins.
He was beaten so we could be whole.
He was whipped so we could be healed.
All of us, like sheep, have strayed away.
We have left God's paths to follow our own.
Yet the Lord laid on him
the sins of us all (Isaiah 53:3-6 NLT).

... this is a gracious thing, when, mindful of God, one endures sorrows while suffering unjustly. For to this you have been called, because Christ also suffered for you, leaving you an example, so that you might follow in his steps. He himself bore our sins in his body on the tree, that we might die to sin and live to righteousness. By his wounds you have been healed (1Peter 2:19,21,24 ESV).

When you are going through something that causes you to look for God and ask why, know this and trust it – you were chosen and equipped for the task.

[1] *[Refers to the Divine Dance of The Trinity]*
Stephen Seamands, *MINISTRY IN THE IMAGE OF GOD* , InterVarsity Press, Downers Grove IL, 2005

Chapter Forty Seven

THE COMMISSION:
NOW – GO
Matthew 28:9-10,16-20

With this climactic passage in Matthew's account, firstly to Israel, I hope to share a little of the joy I've found in the more personal connection, taste and feel of the original context. Reading from the COMPLETE JEWISH BIBLE ©1998 by David H. Stern, the essential words and proper names which are in the language that was and is still spoken, have made it possible to become more familiar with the Hebrew words and pronunciation without having to read Hebrew, and have allowed this reader the increased time in thoughtful engagement, thus deeper insight and impact.

9-10 *Suddenly Yeshua met them and said, "Shalom!" They came up and took hold of his feet as they fell down in front of him. Then Yeshua said to them, "Don't be afraid! Go and tell my brothers to go to the Galil, and they will see me there."*

16-20 *So the eleven talmidim went to the hill in the Galil where Yeshua had told them to go. When they saw him, they prostrated themselves before him; but some hesitated. Yeshua came and talked with them. He said, "All authority in heaven and on earth has been given to me. Therefore, go and make people from all nations into talmidim, immersing them into the reality of the Father, the Son and the Ruach HaKodesh, and teaching them to obey everything that I have commanded you. And remember! I will be with you always, yes, even until the end of the age."* (CJB)

> **Great Commission** – Many call this the "Great Commission" and indeed, that is exactly what it is. But let me urge that we get our definitions and perspective from Jesus, the full scope of His life and message, rather than from sound-byte declarations. That is the strong biblical recommendation in regard to any subject. Get to know Him, He's alive, with us and more capable of communicating His Truth than anyone else. All we have to do is turn from the first impulse being to browse the world's "knowledge" and establish our first, second and third impulse to be, ravenously read His Word, listen for His voice and talk to Him. Then it will be clear what of the world's knowledge is factual and useful.

By this time, having gone through Matthew's record of Jesus' Reality written to a very self-obsessed, stiff-necked people (sound vaguely familiar?), our personal affinities, like Matthew's, may not be as strong a liability as they were before we began. So, we may be less likely to resist pronouncing the Hebrew words and may actually be compelled to look into their definitions. It can be enriching to hear and say aloud the proper names as they are spoken in the language Jesus and His *talmidim* [disciples] actually spoke. To explore our roots as Yeshua's Body-Parts adds meaning and passion to our participation with the One who has been given *"All authority in Heaven and on earth."* His authority is the Cornerstone and Foundation from which He discloses His disciples' full-time, all-consuming occupation. *"Therefore"* we will unpack each element recorded by Matthew with one eye on Mark's account so we can have a three-dimensional view of what Jesus is telling us to do.

Here's a point that I think is interesting because it gives further confirmation to the fact that Jesus always said what He meant and meant exactly what He said. He will always be the Word of God, the genius of God in human flesh and language. Let's get technical:

"Therefore" is the connector in what is called, in *logic,* "entailment," which is a relation between a set of sentences (e.g., meaningfully declarative sentences or <u>truthbearers</u>) and other sentences (Wikipedia).

Jesus set down the declarative, His authority, and then based on that, issued a directive to those who recognized the rock-solid foundational truth of that declarative and would *therefore* be determined and empowered to carry it out.

"All authority in heaven and on earth has been given to me." All authority is a lot. That would mean, whatever His wishes and commands, they would definitely be followed. It stands to reason that those who had witnessed His death and resurrection, the miracles that He performed, as well as His passion for His Father's will and zeal to complete the work He was sent to do, would be eager to hear and follow Jesus' orders.

*"All authority in heaven and on earth has been given to me... Therefore...**Go...**"*

(Because this is the initiating command to action, instead of getting you to look it up in your search engine, I want to share the impact of my own research.)

There's a *"**Go into...**"* (Mark 16:15) but the *"**Go**"* of the Commission given by Jesus to all His disciples, then, now and forever, is first *"**out**,"* then *"**through**."* So the action being called for is more specifically, *"**Go Out and Through**."*

When I asked one of my astute brothers, a student of Torah, about the *"**GO**"*, the first order of the risen Lord's Commission to His disciples, he immediately pointed to a passage echoing Leviticus regarding the instructions for the sin offering, Hebrews 13:11-13:

> *For the bodies of those animals, whose blood is brought into the sanctuary by the high priest for sin, are burned outside the camp. Therefore Jesus also, that He might sanctify the people with His own blood, suffered outside the gate. Therefore let us go forth to Him, outside the camp, bearing His reproach. [NKJ]*

> *For the cohen hagadol brings the blood of animals into the Holiest Place as a sin offering, but their bodies are **burned outside the camp**. So too Yeshua suffered death outside the gate, in order to make the people holy through his own blood. Therefore, let us go out to him who is **outside the camp** and share his disgrace. [CJB]*

Suddenly the light came on! This is the all-knowing, all-powerful, disciple-making nature of Jesus condensing the message of the cross and His Book, in contrast to an Evangelism Drill Sergeant's nature shouting, "What problem do you have with GO? Just get out there!"

"*Go outside the camp,*" outside the walls of our broken-down self, our dogma, our interpretation of what a Christian or a pastor is and what we are. The Fire Jesus will immerse us in, is outside the camp, burning now. He is always calling us out of what we think we know, out into fresh vistas of His reality – "***Come to me***" – to extend our grasp and application of what He designed us for.

In Heaven's perspective, we have **already gone**. We are physically where His design has prescribed. But, only after **going outside our mental/emotional camp to Him,** will we understand what His personal "**go**" means; because then we can see His heart and learn that He has already put us where *He* wants to be. He engineers all of it so He can do what *He* wants to do and be what *He* wants to be – in our skin, for those people He has put us with.

Chapter Forty Eight

THE COMMISSION:
NOW – GO, MAKE
Matthew 28:9-10, 16-20

9-10 Suddenly Yeshua met them and said, "Shalom!" They came up and took hold of his feet as they fell down in front of him. Then Yeshua said to them, "Don't be afraid! Go and tell my brothers to go to the Galil, and they will see me there."

16-20 So the eleven talmidim went to the hill in the Galil where Yeshua had told them to go. When they saw him, they prostrated themselves before him; but some hesitated. Yeshua came and talked with them. He said, "All authority in heaven and on earth has been given to me. Therefore, go and make people from all nations into talmidim, immersing them into the reality of the Father, the Son and the Ruach HaKodesh, and teaching them to obey everything that I have commanded you. And remember! I will be with you always, yes, even until the end of the age." (CJB)

---

*"All authority in heaven and on earth has been given to me... Therefore...****make****..."*

We obey and go out, to **make** disciples. The purpose of following Him out of ourselves is to create in others that same zeal to follow Him which knowing Him has produced in us. God has exclusive prerogative to create, but has graciously extended that activity to involve us as He continued His creative process in the one creation made specifically in His image – *human beings.* We have some specific information about how He creates. He designs and speaks His Design into physical existence. That is the origin of all that we see and know about. He spoke into existence raw material - *something* out of *nothing.* He formed it according to His Design, then breathed life into the creature He spoke into existence. He designs, speaks, breathes.

Personal discovery's fundamental requirement is that we dig right down to the lowest foundation and make sure we build our understanding from there, referring back to the base all along the expedition. God *designed,* then *spoke* the cosmos into existence - out of nothing. [kosmos - ancient Grk =beautiful order, antonyms = void, disorder, chaos] "Let there be..." He **made** Man from the dust of the earth and *breathed* life into him. Basic raw material is created and then molded into whatever the potter designs. In the illustration God gave Jeremiah, the design was marred in the potter's hand (Jeremiah 18). Yes, the original design had the potential to be corrupted, because of a specific faculty inherent in being "*made in the image of God,*" namely, **volition** or free will (see Genesis 1:26).

Certain philosophers concluded that this means the Design is flawed. Not so. That "flaw" is an attribute uniquely God's – thoughtful intentionality with which He purposes to do something, and also acts to perform it. All life is intentional – God's intention is inevitably carried out [no shadow]. Man must *choose* both to *intend* [spirit], as well as to *do* [truth] (see John 4:23).

Now that scientists have mapped the human genome, we can see the "shadow" (see Col 2:17) of the actual spiritual substance and design of Man. That double helix lattice is not the actual spiritual substance, but only the physical machinery (ectoplasmic shadow) of an indestructible, physically-equipped, spiritual being. The first thoroughly spiritual being equipped with a physical body, with all its faculties and facilities, "*fearfully and wonderfully made,*" was *spoken* into existence; *formed,* then *breathed* into by Adonai, the Lord and Life of all His Creation.

To "*make a disciple,*" means to effect a change in the function, focus and force of a person's **volition**; to coax someone out of hiding. We could also say, to awaken the full intention and function of that person. But it is clear, that God's way is to effect that change in the isolated individual without ever abrogating his or her free will. In other words, without coercive domination. The purpose of the serpent's coercive domination over the first Man (in Genesis chapter 3) was to corrupt the inherent "image" of God's nature in the one whom He had created. Of course, that substantive deconstruction altered the physical DNA[1], the shadow of the spiritual creature. The serpent's goal is clear – to spiritually imprison all future human beings in self-conscious isolation from the One in whose image they had been made. Through the Y-chromosome, every following generation inherited that broken DNA[1] with a dead slice, a caved-in portal where full volition and purpose originally pumped vibrant life and inspiration into the whole being.

Why did the Creator create Man impregnated with His image? He was not creating a race in servitude to animal instinct or robotic programming. He wants to have intimate, intentionally unbroken fellowship. So, to regain that original consciousness and connection, servitude to self-conscious isolation must be recognized and overthrown by the individual volition of Man, for it was through free will (though coerced) that it had been corrupted. The person who is making that transition to a life of attention to God's original Design is called, in God's Book, "disciple" [talmid, student]. A friend very close to the development of DISCIPLED, has pointed at our being a part of coaxing someone out of that isolation is a function of participating in the "gravity" of God, drawing them out to Himself, that by impartation of His Gravity to us by the Holy Spirit makes us His human-to-human magnet. That is another beautiful and clear layer of evidence that making a disciple in the sole work of God but that it gloriously includes His personal desire to have us participate as His child's gleefully presented physical body through which He can humanly interact with His targeted candidate.

That life of attending to the original Design will consist of commitment to overcome internal and external resistance, and to practice that Design to the extent that it is being disclosed. It also daily presses in to discover new insight into that Design and enjoy inciting others to make that transition. Enter: you and me, the gone-out ones, on mission.

HOW?

How do I go out, and **make** a disciple? What is the specific participation and influence that a talmid is to exert in that essentially reproductive process?

Because of the baggage we carry (preoccupation with us doing it), the first step in any and every move to follow His lead, is always "**go** out of our broken down self-city to Him", which is both the repentant and obedient action in response to His invitation – "*Come to Me, do what I do, say what I say, step in every footprint I make,*" which means complete trust in and absolute reliance on Jesus the Messiah, the One who does the rescuing and calling. That reliance and trust is based on an ingredient very specifically related to the damage inflicted by the serpent – the broken DNA[2] – which has been passed to every subsequent generation. Jesus was not conceived by sperm containing Yosef's broken DNA. His Y-chromosome was perfect, as Adam's had originally been. Jesus was born a whole human being, of flesh *and* spirit. When He told Nicodemus, "*You must be born again,*" He went on to make His meaning clear. "Physical life can only **make** physical life. Spirit reproduces spiritual life. You must be born of the Spirit." That re-integration gives power to any person who goes out of self and joins forces with Jesus' Spirit in the battle to daily renounce, resist and overthrow the works of the evil one in us. Our indestructible spirit will one day be wrapped in an eternal physical body, but for now, we are armed with His Spirit's resolve to break out of the devil's domination and overcome the residual damage and muscle memory. *That* – is the "work" for which God by His Spirit empowers us. The rest, He alone is able to accomplish.

Mark's gospel gives insight here –

> Mark 16:15-18 – He said to them, *"As you go throughout the world, proclaim the Good News to all creation. Whoever trusts and is immersed will be saved; whoever does not trust will be condemned. And these signs will accompany those who do trust: in my name they will drive out demons, speak with new tongues, not be injured if they handle snakes or drink poison, and heal the sick by laying hands on them."*[3]

Preach the gospel, that is, announce tidings of great joy, a Son is born! The Son of God, Son of Man, the Messiah, He has come! In the vernacular of the Complete Jewish Bible, *"Whoever trusts and is immersed will be saved; whoever does not trust will be condemned."*

> And Luke's account in Acts 1:4-5 – *"Do not leave Jerusalem, but wait for the gift my Father promised, which you have heard me speak about. For John baptized with water, but in a few days you will be baptized with the Holy Spirit...*
>
> 1:8 – *you will receive power when the Holy Spirit comes on you; and you will be my witnesses in Jerusalem, and in all Judea and Samaria, and to the ends of the earth."*
>
> 1:12-14 – *Then the apostles returned to Jerusalem from the hill called the Mount of Olives, a Sabbath day's walk from the city. When they arrived, they went upstairs to the room where they were staying. Those present were Peter, John, James and Andrew; Philip and Thomas, Bartholomew and Matthew; James son of Alphaeus and Simon the Zealot, and Judas son of James. They all joined together constantly in prayer, along with the women and Mary the mother of Jesus, and with his brothers.*

Why did they commit themselves to this determined focus and obedience? Only one thing will cause that. They had seen, touched and been touched by Jesus, Yeshua the Messiah. They had personally witnessed His life, His miracles, His death and His resurrection!

Even after studying and teaching all the methods available today, there is still only one way to "*make disciples*" for Jesus. Introduce them to Him, immerse them in Him, then facilitate their interaction with Him. Take advantage of those divinely scheduled moments with them to model and teach them how to practice living His life in their flesh and bone, nuts and bolts, everyday circumstances. There is only One who can live the life that Jesus described - **Jesus**, living His life in a willing, dedicated soul! [Soul: a spirit expressing itself in a body.]

That's why they committed themselves to that determined focus and obedience. That's the reason anyone in their right mind would commit themself to Him. There are always tangible, physical effects to His physical touch. God's purpose is fulfilled in Jesus, "*I in them, You in me and them in Us*" (John 17:21,23). God found broken yet committed vessels and then... **they heard the Wind and saw the Fire!**

To MAKE DISCIPLES – in action

"*Preach, filled with the Holy Spirit, acknowledging that Yeshua the Messiah came as a human being from God.* (1John4:2)

"*Preach the Word.*" (2 Timothy 4:2)

We are the message. See what God sees and use every power to live it out-loud.

If we lose sight of what God sees, we have forgotten to continually work what we are learning from God out into our fingertips, applying it to our life's practical challenges. "*...not disobedient to the heavenly vision, but openly proclaim to all that they should repent and turn to God, doing deeds and living lives consistent with repentance*" (Acts 26:19-20). His life lived out in us IS the message.

Will we go on following Jesus? Or, will we stop and begin to question when circumstances appear too hard, even impossible, because we can't tell where He is going or what He is doing?

He knows where we are going. He is leading. Following Him is the only way to get there and therefore, the only source of the deep fulfillment and bone-marrow-deep joy that we know we were made for.

KEY: Walk *this minute* in the light He has given *this minute*.

That KEY requires simple action: Look up at Him, our Cornerstone, our bearing.

Gaining and keeping our bearing as a disciple-maker requires being one – **knowing Him** – and knowing Him requires more than a daily dip. It requires being drowned in who He wants to be in this moment, this day, and resurrected to walk through it in Him. His is the full functionality He will employ in dealing with the specific situations, circumstances and people He has designed in our day. He will deal with it personally by walking us through each one clothed in our skin.

Our God is a consuming fire.

[1] Douglas M Hamp, *CORRUPTING THE IMAGE,* CreateSpace Independent Publishing Platform, 2013

Chapter Forty Nine

THE COMMISSION:
NOW – GO, MAKE, **IMMERSE**
Matthew 28:9-10, 16-20

⁹⁻¹⁰ Suddenly Yeshua met them and said, "Shalom!" They came up and took hold of his feet as they fell down in front of him. Then Yeshua said to them, "Don't be afraid! Go and tell my brothers to go to the Galil, and they will see me there."

¹⁶⁻²⁰ So the eleven talmidim went to the hill in the Galil where Yeshua had told them to go. When they saw him, they prostrated themselves before him; but some hesitated. Yeshua came and talked with them. He said, "All authority in heaven and on earth has been given to me. Therefore, go and make people from all nations into talmidim, immersing them into the reality of the Father, the Son and the Ruach HaKodesh, and teaching them to obey everything that I have commanded you. And remember! I will be with you always, yes, even until the end of the age." (CJB)

> Alert: To communicate the continuity and fullness of these subjects may require the use of compound sentences and dismembered words. So, let's take courage and do not tire in exercising our minds; don our concentration caps and build each picture, line-upon-line.

*"All authority in heaven and on earth has been given to me.... Therefore...**immerse**..."*

The Greek word is commonly translated in English versions, "baptize." However, baptism communicates varied concepts in religious culture, most of which refer to unexplained ritual. That multiplies the possible inferences by a number at least equal to the number of people attending the baptism (except one, in some settings, who only feels the sensation of something wet on their head). But the original definitions of the words God uses are important because it is His infinite mind, His all-encompassing Truth that is to be conveyed to, rather than defined by, *our* finite minds.

"*The fear* [out of reverence and awe] *of* [misrepresenting, offending] *the Lord is the beginning of knowledge*" (Proverbs 1:7 conglomerate amplification, sum of respected exposition of "fear of the Lord")

To make *talmidim* of fallen people begins with a relentless discipline of attention to God's specific meaning when He speaks. *And God said, "Let there be light, and there was light."* When God is speaking, He is creating. What He is creating is specific. Investigating the specific, in High Definition, begins to open our limited minds to this boundless Person and shed light on the meaning of the fathomless insights He desires to share. He daily remodels our minds by pouring in more of Himself. Each morning He has graciously prepared a bath specifically for us to step into and be completely immersed in the pure atmosphere of the Living Water and the Breath He breathes, to infuse our hungry soul with "*all that pertains to* our *life and godliness*" today. (2Peter1:3) "His *mercies and loving kindness are new every morning*" (Lamentations 3:22-23). His presence, that consuming fire, is death to all that is not found in Him, thus healing the very core of our hearts, which He alone can touch. Our love for Him and utter trust compels us to expectantly lay aside the clothes [self] of yesterday and step into that total transformation for a new day. (see Ephesians 4)

To be immersed is a foundational element in the work of Redemption, but unfortunately was only partially understood and applied before Jesus showed up, even though this tenet was daily illustrated and practiced in the Jewish bathing instructions[1]. Remember what Yohanan the Immerser said, "*It is true that I am immersing you in water so that you might turn from sin to God; but the one coming after me is more powerful than I and he will immerse you in the Ruach HaKodesh and in fire*" (Matt 3:11). What John is saying is exactly what Jesus says in Matt 16:19, "*... immersing them into the reality of the Father, the Son and the Ruach HaKodesh.*"

Hang on. John says "*the Coming One [Jesus] will immerse...*" Jesus says, "*You, [my talmadim] will immerse...*" Jesus repeatedly teaches and implements this pivotal transfer of personal action from Himself to His disciples during His time with them. Then, as if to provide further revelation and training in this completely foreign concept to isolated self-imprisoned humans, He knocks Saul of Tarsus down in the road to Damascus opening a heavenly window and focusing His blinding light on him. Next day He opens his eyes, transforms his identity, strips him of his dogma and takes him out into the desert. (Reminds me of how He dealt with Moses when he was so eager to put God's plan into play *his* way, in Exodus 3.) With Saul in the desert, He opens up the mystery of building a human mega-Body for Himself to this young man who, from childhood, had been so immersed in the Words of God that he was likely to be the next super-rabbi. The revelation is, "The Father is *in* Me – I am *in* the Father – We come and make our home *in* you. **NOW** – you are *in* Us – I am the Head – you are my Body Parts. Each Part is endued with an aspect of My manifold Personality and Functionality, distributed to all who are Mine, physically walking among people all over the whole earth. I, *in* you, your hope of glory." [Glory in Scripture means direct performance of the unseen God in the tangible, visible and audible universe, which He created for that purpose.] That is you and I, if we will but establish the simple habit of coming to Him, living our daily lives with/in Him. We, together, are His physical presence – "The Word, made flesh [IN US] and walking among" broken human beings, on His mission to talk to them, and to tear away the veil which isolates them from the reality of a Life lived to His glory.

This brings to mind the parallel instructions for husbands who are to love their wives as Jesus loves His Church, "...and washes her daily in the pure Water of the Word (Ephesians 5)." As a disciple-maker, we make sure washing in that Living Water is a daily occurrence, along with asking the Spirit for wisdom to apply every word.

To *IMMERSE* – in action

First – Be immersed

Second – Be the immersion. Starting each day having been immersed in what Jesus pours into us for this day, He loads us with all that He wants to pour into those He gives us to.

[For full background, look up **Mikveh** in your search engine.]

Chapter Fifty

THE COMMISSION:
NOW – GO, MAKE, IMMERSE, **TEACH**
Matthew 28:9-10, 16-20

The mind of God is clearly HIS mind and foreign to our stunted perception of reality. We must be TAUGHT/TRAINED to apply His mind and make it ours.

Immersion in water, illustrating express, personal separation from the world and abandon to God, is a strong public statement to family and acquaintances of the covenant with God that has been privately entered into by the one being immersed. It is clear, from John the Immerser's distinction between what he was doing and what Jesus would soon come to do, that immersion in water is only a public proclamation of death to the old life and entry into the perpetually refreshed life of faith that, "*believe and be immersed,*" always referred to.

All the ecclesiastical wrestling since those words were written in Mark's gospel is about questions, which could only have existed between the time John began baptizing and Pentecost. Arguing issues that were cleared from the list of unsolved mysteries the day the Holy Spirit drowned the apostles in the liquid fire of Heaven's atmosphere, is frivolous. There was no question what Jesus meant by "immersing" in His instructions just before they watched Him rise from where He was standing till the clouds obscured their view. The cloud that had obscured their understanding of Jesus' words up to that day was suddenly and completely swept away by the Breath of God just a few days later. A mighty Wind shook the house and separated to Himself the sacrificial bodies of those obedient, now abandoned to God, emissaries of His agenda in the world.

This is a fitting threshold for the admonition to TEACH, because the preparatory stage for "to TEACH" is a data-dump, an upload of new, revolutionary data. A new software installation requires full system activation and training to assure its successful performance, an apt illustration for what Jesus is referring to as, "teaching". It is not enough to install a new OS. There must be someone who has preceded the student in that process and has been given the tools and authority to provide an active tutorial, contextually and practically – theory and lab – until the student becomes proficient in the pursuit of Jesus' life on duty, fully integrated and in authority. The most effective teacher is the one who operates with the understanding that it must be an interactive task with hands-on practice and experimentation. To just go on and on verbally repeating and expounding on the elements of the new OS to a (hopefully) listening class can hardly be called teaching.

These very motivated students, the disciples of Jesus, had done exactly what the Teacher instructed them to do – stay and wait. *LAB is coming!*

> *He, who says God gives no specific instruction,*
> *reveals his intentional ignorance.* [Anon]

Matthew 28:9-10, 16-20

9-10 Suddenly Yeshua met them and said, "Shalom!" They came up and took hold of his feet as they fell down in front of him. Then Yeshua said to them, "Don't be afraid! Go and tell my brothers to go to the Galil, and they will see me there."

16-20 So the eleven talmidim went to the hill in the Galil where Yeshua had told them to go. When they saw him, they prostrated themselves before him; but some hesitated. Yeshua came and talked with them. He said, "All authority in heaven and on earth has been given to me. Therefore, go and make people from all nations into talmidim, immersing them into the reality of the Father, the Son and the Ruach HaKodesh, and teaching them to obey everything that I have commanded you. And remember! I will be with you always, yes, even until the end of the age." (CJB)

---

*"All authority in heaven and on earth has been given to me... Therefore...***teach***..."*

Bet Midrash- 1. Teach 2. Instruct 3. Train 4. Practice 5. Indoctrinate [For full background, look up **Bet Midrash** in your search engine.]

Actual teaching is very scarce in the current world. It is happening, but it takes deep conviction and determination in the teacher to establish it.

"Indoctrination by the illusion of license" is one way I would describe the common mode of "education" today, not only in the public schools and universities, but also in churches. We've built our churches like theaters so as not to challenge the illusion of personal sovereignty [individuality] even as the whole counsel of God is being expounded from the elevated sacred desk. Any genuine educator will tell us, the goal of teaching is learning, and learning must come through experience and be verifiable. It is profound truth for the teacher to say, "This chemical, mixed with that one will produce an odious billow of smoke." It is quite another thing to actually mix those chemicals in a beaker and have that smoke billow into your face. This is a good illustration of the mission of the "gifts" God has given to the Body of Christ (see Ephesians 5). That mission is to build and equip the Saints – for what? For their particular part of the ministry Jesus is doing through His flesh-and-blood Body-parts to those He puts them with. That is Heaven's version of church-growth. The goal is to equip and train people for the work Jesus has specifically given *them*, in the home and workplace where He has put *them*, with every attribute of His disposition active and yielded to *in them*.

To stand in an elevated pulpit in a room, speaking to people who are only allowed to listen and not encouraged to interact, or openly mix the chemicals at the lab-table and react appropriately to the explosion, may be a lot of things but it is not "teaching." No matter how stirring the message, the truth about what is actually being assimilated would quickly be discovered through a potentially embarrassing tally of answers to questions about Christian basics as people exit the building on Sunday morning. Instead, we finance elaborate "church-growth" studies to find out why "the church" is so lethargic; why new Christians are so quickly lukewarm; and why so many young people depart from faith in God as soon as they enter college.

The answer is as clear as the nose on our face. Every time the double-scalpel of God's Word is opened, it does surgery on the human heart. With no closing on the surgical table, recovery room care, or re-training, the patients are dismissed with open incisions and sent home to sew themselves up and try to make sense of why they are developing layer after layer of scar tissue. Why a lethargic, apathetic congregation? Clue: there are no nerve endings in scar tissue, but there is often debilitating pain internally from frayed nerves trapped by that scar tissue.

For the entirety of the first Century, the Church was Jewish in nationality and culture, devout lovers of Torah and faithful synagogue gatherers, often joined by gentile "God-fearers". The synagogue and family living rooms were the models of the 1st Century Church, not the Greek lecture hall nor the Roman theater. In synagogue or someone's home, everyone was there to participate in the experiments with the elements that Torah put on the Lab-Table, Bema Seat. Everyone was seen and heard and it was brought to a new, even higher level of engagement by the power of the Blood of the Lamb and then, the work of His Spirit, to draw all people into fellowship with Him and with each other!

Of course we cannot fathom how we could manage that, having grown up in the kind of churches common since the 4th Century AD; thanks to Constantine. Even with the parade of "rock show technology" and "novel" twists through the years, it hasn't wandered very far from the controlled environment of the entertainment of theatre or the listening, note taking lecture hall.

On hearing this kind of talk, the common questioning rebuttal from teaching pastors and church leaders is, "How can that be feasible now?" They may have come to class expecting the new Clark Method, 5-step transformation plan, or honestly wanting to know, but my only possible answer is, "I'm not the one to ask and neither should we ask "church-growth experts." The one we will have to risk asking is Jesus. It's His Church and I'm sure He's the only one who knows how to grow those particular people and make them functional and fruitful. I can't tell someone else exactly how He will want to do it in the flock He has given them to, but I can guarantee that if they are willing to ask Him, with real determination to do what He instructs, it will certainly change things. Then comes the common woeful cry, "But, we've worked so hard to get it the way it is!"

I can with confidence also predict that the Head of the Church's instructions will look a lot like, "GO out of the gates of your walled self-city to Me, and we'll MAKE disciples by IMMERSing people in everything I am, TEACHing them to apply Me to every aspect of their daily life and to REMEMBER, I'm right there." But, the "TEACH" will consist of faithfully bathing Jesus' interactive Body-parts in His eternally-right-now Word, AND guiding and training them to be intimately connected to Jesus; and together work that out into the work-a-day, common life He has given *them*. The pastor's job is first leading the way, then guiding them as they learn to become willing host bodies for His nature, His wisdom, His instructions, to those He has sent them to live with and bless. Equipping the saints for the work of the ministry means immersing them in everything Jesus is, and training them to apply who He is in them to every situation, every conversation, every relationship in the daily life He has laid out for them. It means training them to GO out of themselves and MAKE disciples with Jesus, gathering and IMMERSING them in everything they're coming to know about Him; and TEACHING, training them to surrender their body for His agenda in the other lives He has put them with, while remembering He is always close. In fact He is right there in intimate fellowship with them, clothing Himself in their skin, involving them in the work He wants to do in those He connects them with.

> The world's marketing schemes and bright ideas cannot produce *that* kind of multiplication and coordinated function, nor can they stop it!

The final key to being a functional part of that ever-flowing, perpetually fruitful work of God is to REMEMBER. We practice remembering that Jesus is right here in us and that it is His work He has enlisted us for. We are each, one of the millions of His Flesh & Blood Boots-on-the-ground around the world, in whom He is alive and at home. Each one of us is carrying a vital facet of His limitless personality, which is designed specifically for that place, those people, moving in sync with the other parts. He is HUGE! His master plan is to "shed abroad," distribute Himself, in human beings abandoned to Him, to serve at His pleasure, now and forever. Memory comes with practice and practice makes perfect.

Chapter Fifty One

The COMMISSION:
NOW – GO, MAKE, IMMERSE, TEACH &
REMEMBER
Matthew 28:9-10, 16-20

⁹⁻¹⁰ Suddenly Yeshua met them and said, "Shalom!" They came up and took hold of his feet as they fell down in front of him. Then Yeshua said to them, "Don't be afraid! Go and tell my brothers to go to the Galil, and they will see me there."

¹⁶⁻²⁰ So the eleven talmidim went to the hill in the Galil where Yeshua had told them to go. When they saw him, they prostrated themselves before him; but some hesitated. Yeshua came and talked with them. He said, "All authority in heaven and on earth has been given to me. Therefore, go and make people from all nations into talmidim, immersing them into the reality of the Father, the Son and the Ruach HaKodesh, and teaching them to obey everything that I have commanded you. And remember! I will be with you always, yes, even until the end of the age." (CJB)

"All authority in heaven and on earth has been given to me... Therefore... **remember***..."*

Jesus' last specific instruction to His disciples before He disappears from physical view, is *REMEMBER*. Like the previous instructions, Jesus has expanded and revised each individual concept. Yes, He defines WHAT can be remembered, but He also gives a completely new and creative HOW His ever-presence can be remembered. Remembrance of the miraculous events would be impossible to delete from their minds. Blind eyes had been opened, lepers were cleansed, and the dead were raised to life. The list would go on and on. One of them said, *"The books needed to record it all would fill the whole world (John 21:25)!"*

Those events were etched eternally in their audio, visual and emotional memories. Jesus would not need to say, and therefore, would not say, "Remember all that you've seen me do." They will never forget a single detail of what they saw Him do. No, He said, *"Always remember, I am with you."* That adds dimension to, *"As often as you eat and drink together, do it remembering I'm right there at the table with you, as I am now."*

The HOW or nature of that remembrance is the completely new concept. *"Behold!"* is the actual meaning of the word translated *"Remember."* So, *"Pay attention!"* Yochanan ben-Zavdai [John son of Zebedee] records Jesus teaching them that, in chapters 14-17 of his journal. *"In a little while the world will no longer see Me. But you will see Me. The Father is sending the Spirit of Truth to you and He will remind you and teach you all that I have said to you. I will not leave you orphans. I am coming to you. I will be in you. I'm leaving you my Shalom (John 14:25-27)."*

So, *"REMEMBER"* is actually, "Practice, make a habit of being aware that I'm never absent from you and therefore be engaged in our fellowship in all that is happening, as the Holy Spirit reminds you and trains you how to apply everything I've told you. Then, together, we will get done what we were meant to accomplish in this age – by our combined, flesh-and-blood presence, relationships and actions." A pivotal component of remembering God, is the understanding of faith, or trust, in Him, as revealed in His Book and imparted by Him. The human compulsion to categorize types of circumstances and events as being from God or Satan or human initiation, is a delusional and regressive mutation of, and has no part with, God's fully revealed and precisely articulated definition of faith. Human beings are broken and, by definition, have no discernment of reality outside of the sovereign creativity of God and the all-encompassing, infinite knowledge of His mind, as revealed by His Spirit. He is absolutely, the ONLY source of ANYTHING we come in contact with, mentally, spiritually or physically.

I am sure we can, by a short review of human history, eventually come to agreement that it is completely irrational to suppose that Man could be the sole creative source of anything, anywhere. There seems to be a more formidable barrier though, to agreement that Satan absolutely does NOT possess creative power, no matter how much he does to convince us to think that. Contrary to his marketing, THE DEVIL IS NOT GOD'S EQUAL AND OPPOSITE COMPETITOR! Nor, God help us, is he the dark side of the same life-regulating force!! The devil, the serpent, is a creature, a created being who is dark only because of the intentional rejection and thus, the utter absence of Light. Darkness has no substance. Darkness only occupies space or beings because light has been blocked or filtered. Anything or anyone who thinks themselves sovereignly creative is delusional, either because they are a simpleton, or the voluntary slave of the "father of all lies," or both. Neither has the capacity to tell a truth. There is one exception – the devil makes use of truth, which he knows perfectly well, to cloak his lie, to assist its penetration into the heart of the simpleton, thus, the aptly fitting description – diabolical!

While we might intellectually agree with those statements, too often we fall for the seduction to categorize circumstances and events by giving credit to the devil for something God did. That's deadly, according to Jesus (see Matt 12:27-32). He said there is one unforgiveable breach of faith – ascribing to the devil what God is doing. How does someone distinguish between the acts of God and the acts of the devil? Whose criteria are used? I can hear the guess-and-fake-it philosophical argument for the common basis of that judgment, "God is good, right? The devil is bad, right? So, the good stuff is obviously God's doing and the bad stuff is the devil's doing." Sounds right enough, until you read God's Book and find out *God* is God, even of the definition of "GOOD;" gross over-trivialization, to say the least. Hasn't God used a RED LIGHT in His work in our lives just as many times as He's used a GREEN LIGHT? It is possible that if we are honest and our memory is "good," we'll probably be able to count many more RED LIGHTS than GREEN.

The trustworthy promise He is fulfilling every minute of every day is "God is working *all* things together for the "good" of those who love Him and walk after the dictates of the Spirit." (see Rom 8:28).
ALL is a big little word. So, let's summarize:
- ✓ Nothing is created by the devil.
  - ○ Satan can only add a deluding lie to the creativity of God.
- ✓ God has created everything.
  - ○ He is working all together for the good of those who love Him.
- ✓ So, our job is to REMEMBER.
  - ○ See and acknowledge ALL things as from His good-working hand.
- ✓ Don't credit the devil for something of which he is not even remotely capable.

- Take notice of the continuity of God's working all things together all day, every day.
  - ✓ That will lift our eyes to see the good thing He is creating.
    - More good news: What He starts, He finishes.

To "*REMEMBER*" is therefore the verification of being on course; the looking up and aligning everything that is going on, with the Cornerstone. It is truly a beautiful life He gives us who love Him so completely that we live entirely for His pleasure. We never have to guess and fake anything. He, the Way, the Truth, the Life, the answer to every question, is with us. "Don't be troubled, I'M RIGHT HERE!!"

THERE'S A CHOICE

If you sense, as you read these words, that any of them are spoken directly to you, you may have, to some degree, already responded positively to Jesus' underlying call to you personally, "*Come to Me*" in that particular. If you choose to accept His Commission, your orders have been made clear. But it is *His* work, so, for the orders to be understood and activated, specific preparation is required. Wait, optimally with others that are also accepting the Commission, and you will be given a complete install, verification and launch of a new Operating System. The OS is installed so that God's own Personality can be the Operating System, fully functional and in sync with Himself in all the Body-Parts in the world, though – we do not make that our focus of attention without obscuring our view of Him and missing His slightest suggestion. He will train and equip you to completely release your life *to Him*. Remember, He does the ministry. We give our concentrated attention so that we do not get distracted and lose sight of His work in each of us, as we – GO, MAKE, IMMERSE, TEACH and REMEMBER.

Chapter Fifty Two

CONCLUSION

During the 1st Century AD, Roman soldiers prophetically gave us the nickname, Christianos, intending it to be used as a prejudicial slur. It is the Greek word for Messiah, Anointed One, with a Latin term tacked on to denote "adhering to" or "belonging to, as a slave." As Christians, our life is His life – His purpose is alive in our surrendered body, going and doing what He originally designed us for – FOREVER. What does that look like? It looks like us, unexceptional normal us, loyally doing what He daily puts in our hands to do, with unsurpassed joy and contentment. We engage and interact with whatever happens, knowing that He has designed it all for infinite layers of purpose which we will only perceive as He chooses to open and unpack them for us.

There are no class distinctions or levels of Christians in God's Book, only unique, yet functionally interlinked, participants in His work. A person is either a Christian – a bond-slave of Jesus – or not. There are always choices. I guess what I'm saying is, there's no such thing as a partial or sort-of Christian. If we are accused of being a Christian, I would hope and pray the accuser has the evidence to prove it.

Those who seek guidelines for hands-on action, might ask, "So, when does the disciple-making begin?" Let me be defibrillator-paddle-clear, Jesus abhors flesh-hook theatrics, religious airs and emotionally charged coercion under the banner of "the work of the Holy Spirit". Jesus says, "You can say whatever you will about me and be forgiven, but misrepresenting the Holy Spirit will never be forgiven." (see Mark 3:28-30 + footnote AMP) It can be a lucrative "business," but could be deadly to all who attribute it to the Ruach HaKodesh.

The tool in the Holy Spirit's hand is that unpretentious, all-in, humble life described throughout Matthew's journal. That is the most powerful expression of the life of Jesus in a human being. I wonder if we can bring ourselves to connect that with Jesus' version of "making disciples" and lose the mind-set that envisions someone with an office, on staff at a church or a conference speaker with the title that suggests expertise in the work of "Discipling." That is prevalent because we want to be significant to people as well as tabulate our success and use that record to market and build our influence.

Being in a vital, passionate, transforming relationship with Jesus every day will express itself in everything we say and do. The Spirit will touch, He will love, and He will heal the people He puts us with because of our ever-deepening loyalty to Jesus. Every conversation we have with Him will always be fresh and ready, audibly on our lips and present in our bearing, our work. That will be so, not because we decided, "This is the method, so I will work on doing that," but because He is really that good and He's blowing our mind with intimate insights that completely remodel our life every day! That is preaching most fruitful, because He is, not just *a* king but, ***The* King** wielding *His* influence and authority to affect human beings.

The beauty and holiness of our Almighty, Sovereign King surpasses any need to market our vocation as disciples. Being completely engaged in the active personal interaction with the King Himself, overshadows all our attention to the effect we may be having on those around us. Essentially, a true disciple will be the last one to notice enough of the full effect of what the Spirit is doing to even think of taking credit. What the Spirit does will simply explode through our physical presence, because He is personally presenting a live (unmanufactured) projection of what He wants to communicate.

If Jesus is being glorified in me, He will be glorified through me, with or without my conscious awareness of it. He is the One performing *His* will in my will – *His* creativity – *His* fruit – *His* joy – *His*. In light of the explosion required to blast human beings out of their pet prisons, my most fruitful action is to get *my self* hidden so deeply in Him that I am out of the way.

> Here is a mash-up of several quotes to give insight into two aspects of "make":
> God is a consuming fire. When we are set aflame with His passion, people naturally gather round to warm themselves and watch us burn. Pray the fire spreads and the Lord of the Harvest sends more burning coals into the dark and cold world, until the whole world believes.

REMINDER

Many call this the "Great Commission" and indeed, that is exactly what it is. But let us be reminded again to get our definitions and perspectives directly from Jesus, the full scope of His life and message, rather than from clever sound-bytes. That is the Holy Spirit's strong recommendation in regard to any subject. Get to know Him. He is alive and more capable of communicating His Truth to us and through us than anyone else. He is also right here with each of us. All we have to do is discard the first impulse being to browse the world's "knowledge" and establish our first, second and third impulse to ravenously read His Word, listen for His voice and talk to Him. It will then be clear what of the world's knowledge is in truth factual and useful.

Made in the USA
Monee, IL
29 January 2021

59101063R00125